WILD SWIMMING IN IRELAND

DISCOVER 50 PLACES TO SWIM
IN RIVERS, LAKES & THE SEA

Swimming is a risk sport. The authors and The Collins Press accept no responsibility for any injury, loss or inconvenience sustained by anyone using this guidebook.

Life ring on the horseshoe strand of Dog's Bay, County Galway

WILD SWIMMING IN IRELAND

DISCOVER 50 PLACES TO SWIM IN RIVERS, LAKES & THE SEA

Maureen McCoy and Paul McCambridge

The Collins Press

FIRST PUBLISHED IN 2016 BY
The Collins Press
West Link Park
Doughcloyne
Wilton
Cork
T12 N5EF
Ireland

Reprinted in 2021

A CIP record for this book is available from the British Library.

Paperback ISBN: 978-1-84889-280-4

Design and typesetting by Burns Design
Typeset in San Francisco and Generis
Printed by Hussar Books, Poland

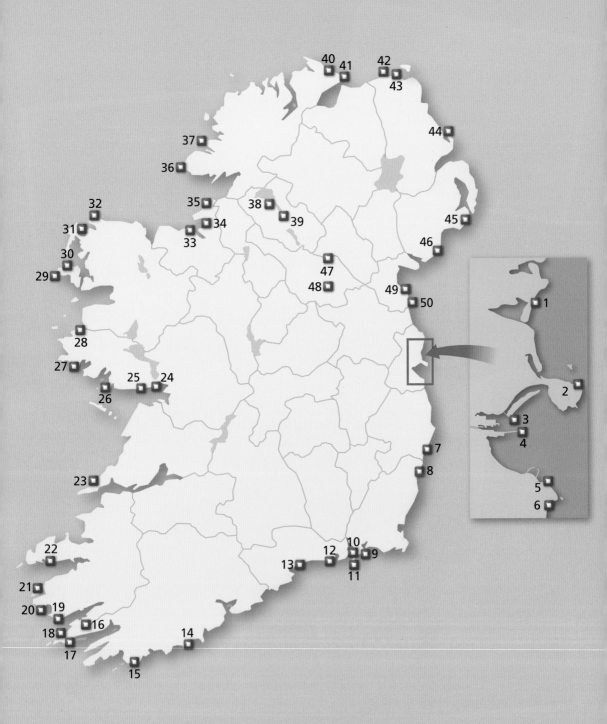

Contents

INTRODUCTION

If your idea of a great day at the beach is to lie beside a few hundred others with jet skis beating up and down the shore, put this book down now... BUT, if that is your idea of a nightmare and you wish to get away from the hordes, discover forgotten coves to swim, picnic and play in, then this book is for you.

Wild Swimming in Ireland is an introductory guide to wild swimming around the country. Journeying from county to county, it takes you on a swimming adventure exploring the countryside and coast, searching for hidden gems and forgotten treasures: swim under the Carrick-a-Rede Rope Bridge on the rugged coast of Ulster where the chilly North Sea challenges swimmers and kayakers; circumnavigate Devenish Island in the fresh waters of Lough Erne waterways; travel along Ireland's Wild Atlantic Way, Europe's longest designated coastal route to explore the beautiful hidden beaches and coves; visit Galway, famed for vibrant music sessions that go on all night and plunge from the dual-aspect high-diving boards or do a spot of beachcombing at the multicoloured Coral Beach.

City swimming in Dublin is popular. We show you our favourite places to go, from Donabate to the Forty Foot. Journey to the beaches of the sunny south-east and explore the rock pool at Hook Head Lighthouse. Head south to Waterford's rugged Copper Coast, then strike west for the dramatic peninsulas of Kerry.

Ireland has much varied swimming to offer. Whether you are a keen swimmer, a curious observer or an armchair swimmer, one of the growing number of triathletes and long-distance swimmers, or a grandparent introducing grand-children to the pleasures of the sea, this book will inspire and enlighten you.

Those who simply want to play and explore will find a wonderful guide to the waters in and around Ireland and excellent tips.

Note: Distances are given in kilometres throughout but we have added miles in Northern Irish counties, as you will encounter road signs in miles there.

SAFE SWIMMING

Outdoor swimming is a great year-round sport and growing fast in popularity, but this is not the controlled environment of the swimming pool. There are often no lifeguards, the shore may be further away than you think and the water is much cooler: the average public pool temperature is around 27–28 °C while the average sea temperature around Ireland ranges from 8 °C to 18 °C. Add to that wind chill and water movement and in February temperatures can get really low (I have personally recorded swims at 3 °C!). Lakes tend to warm up and cool down more quickly than sea water, some getting to icy depths in winter.

If you can swim, you can swim outdoors; just as with any other outdoor activity, wild swimming is only dangerous if swimmers take unnecessary risks. Common sense and a little preparation can make it safe and fun.

Remember that outdoor conditions – rain, wind, the tides, ambient temperatures – change all the time. You will never have the same swim twice. This is why swimmers keep coming back for more, because wild swimming is never boring!

KNOW YOUR LIMITS

Know your own swimming ability, how well you can function in the cold, your knowledge of currents, tides and your ability to read the conditions. If you are less confident, stay within your depth and close to an easy exit point.

NEVER SWIM ALONE

The number one rule of swimming: always swim with a buddy. It gives you each a safety backup and it is more fun as a shared experience.

SEEK ADVICE

In an unfamiliar area, ask advice about conditions, water quality, hazards or currents. Tide tables are readily available to download to your phone and can be saved for a quick check. Keep an eye on the weather: sunshine where you are does not necessarily mean it will be sunny and calm where you intend to swim.

NEVER DIVE INTO UNFAMILIAR WATER

Always check the depth and for any obstacles. Cold-water shock can debilitate the strongest of swimmers (it can even cause loss of consciousness). It is better to walk in slowly, acclimatise and settle your breathing. Then you can swim to your heart's content.

BE VISIBLE

Wear a bright swimming cap to make yourself visible to any craft in the area. All that will be obvious is your tiny head, which any wave more than a few inches high will hide, and your flying arms – unless you breast stroke, in which case only your head will be visible. At approximately 500 metres your head will be no more than a small dot to any other water traffic.

SWIM PARALLEL TO SHORE

You can get back to safety more easily if you swim parallel to shore than if you swim straight out to sea or to the middle of a lake. On point-to-point swims, try to choose markers that keep you close to shore.

FOOD AND DRINK

Never swim within two hours of a meal and NEVER after ANY alcohol.

WATCH THE WEATHER

Do not try to swim in rough conditions: no matter how strong you think you are, the water is always more powerful. It is very difficult to breathe or navigate in choppy water. In fog you will lose your bearings and will not be visible to others.

KEEP WARM

Body temperature drops extremely quickly in the water and after swimming you may experience a further drop. Be sure to have warm clothes to change into and a warm drink after your swim.

TELL OTHERS

If there is someone on shore, tell them your swimming plans: say where you are going and when you plan to return.

RIVER SWIMMING

If you are intending to do an out-and-back swim it is best to head upstream first, so that you return with the flow of the river helping you. It is surprising how what may seem like very little current can be extremely difficult to counter, especially when you are tired.

BE AWARE OF THE COLD

Recent findings show that around 60 per cent of drownings in Britain and Ireland are due to Cold-Shock Response, the immediate physical response to sudden cold, which causes involuntary inhalation. In waters around 15 °C it is extremely difficult for even strong swimmers to hold their breath when suddenly immersed.

It takes an inhalation of only 1.5 litres of water to drown an adult.

The solution? DO NOT jump straight in – no matter how inviting the water looks. Instead, follow the ritual of most seasoned outdoor swimmers: get in slowly, wet your arms and face, lower yourself in gently, swim head up at first to acclimatise and control your breathing. Then, once you are no longer gasping or out of breath, you may put your head down and speed off.

The inclination may to be to charge down the beach on that scorching first day of spring and dive head first into the inviting water; just take your time.

For more comprehensive information check out:
http://www.coldwatersafety.org/nccwsRules3.html#

ESSENTIAL KIT

A SENSE OF ADVENTURE!

All outdoor swimmers have a little rebel streak in them. Celebrate that and enjoy the exploration of new places, or old ones seen from a new perspective.

SWIM SENSE

It seems tedious to reiterate but use your noggin! If your gut feeling is that it is a bad idea, it probably is. Confidence is all very well but competence is key: know your own limitations in swimming ability and your capacity to deal with the cold. Seek advice from others and start gently, and enjoy building your confidence, skill and power in the water.

DRY CLOTHING

After a swim your body temperature will drop, so get dried and dressed quickly. Too many layers are better than too few.

DESIRABLE KIT

SWIMSUIT

Essential at popular beaches, although there are plenty of places where this is optional.

GOGGLES

Great for seeing clearly underwater, keeping your eyeballs from feeling as if they are going to freeze and generally for seeing where you are going. They have a nasty habit of steaming up, though, so prepare them beforehand (rub with a smear of baby shampoo then wipe dry) or a generous amount of spit may be required.

CAP

Keeps hair out of the eyes, can help minimise water in the ears (when pulled down enough) and provides a layer of insulation (there are times when you will be glad of that few millimetres of silicone). Caps come in a range of types, styles and, of course, colours. If sea swimming, go for bright neon colours that are more likely to be seen. Silicone caps beat latex for thickness and insulation and are less likely to tear. Neoprene hoods tend to be favoured by triathletes and some winter swimmers as they give more insulation but swimmers used to caps may find the chinstrap inhibiting.

CHANGING TOWEL

Keeps you decent on busy beaches and provides something of a windbreak. There are many on the market and budget is your only limitation – I still love my trusty handcrafted version, modelled on the ones Mum made for my brothers and me when we were small.

HOT-WATER BOTTLE

Part of my essential winter kit, either already filled, with my socks tucked inside the cover (heavenly!) or a spare flask of hot water ready to fill it when I get out.

FLASK OF HOT BEVERAGE

Smooth, creamy and indulgent hot chocolate is a popular choice but any hot drink is a great way to warm up after a swim. Most will accompany this with a sweet snack.

DRY BAG

A large dry bag for your towels and dry clothes, and a small dry bag for car keys (I personally like to double-bag my key and bring it with me – just in case – and I always keep a spare towel, fleece and jogging bottoms in the car, in case someone thinks it funny to nick my gear from the beach).

THERMAL UNDIES

Not the most flattering but they are simply great.

VERY WARM BOOTS

For after the swim, especially winter swims, a fleece-lined boot you can pull on is oh so nice – you can stuff disposable hand warmers into your socks, too.

OPTIONAL EXTRAS

WETSUIT

Wetsuits provide a great deal of insulation and some buoyancy. Thanks to the rising popularity of triathlon and open-water swimming there is now a good range of affordable wetsuits. Try before you buy. If you are going to use it mostly for swimming do get a swim/triathlon specific suit. The heavy surfing-type wetsuits may keep you warm but do not have the flexibility around the arms and shoulders to allow for the increased freedom of movement swimmers need. Many swimmers find the necklines tight on wetsuits so get used to the suit before you head out for your epic swim. Be aware that purists may call you a 'wimp'. If you are already a wetsuit swimmer, next time you are out take a few minutes at the end of your swim to cast aside the suit and try a quick dip in just your swimsuit – you might just love it!

NEOPRENE BOOTIES
Extremely useful if you are likely to be clambering over rocks for good grip and to protect delicate skin.

MASK, SNORKEL, FINS
Great fun for exploring the underwater world. There is a surprising array of sea creatures to see in Ireland's clear waters. Fins can give you a lot of speed and if they fit well you can catch more waves to bodysurf.

WATERPROOF CAMERA
Great for documenting your swimming adventure. Beware, though, of taking those 'arty' pics half under and half above the water – your subject may not find the resulting image entirely flattering!

HAND WARMERS
Disposable ones are warmer but the reusable ones are a little more environmentally friendly – a hot-water bottle may do the same job. There is a wealth of other gear on the market – gloves, swim floats, lifebuoys – the choice is yours.

TOW FLOATS
Tow floats are NOT life-saving equipment so do not rely on them. They do, however, make a swimmer much more visible to other water traffic. They can also be used if you need a short rest on a long swim but remember that your temperature will drop very quickly when you are inactive in the water. Some of these floats are designed to carry a drinks bottle: useful when doing long training swims.

GLOW STICKS
For night swimming, tucked into the goggle strap, these allow others to see the swimmer.

The most important piece of equipment you have is yourself – your own competence and judgment.

BEST REASONS TO SWIM OUTDOORS

'Going swimming' now means a day trip to the beach or lake or mountains with a warm-up drink and scone after, or, better still, the pub where you can cosy up to the fire while sipping Guinness.

BOOSTS THE IMMUNE SYSTEM

This is not yet backed up by medical evidence but any year-round swimmer will tell you that when they swim through the winter they simply don't get a cold.

FEEL-GOOD FACTOR

Undoubtedly the best reason for doing it is that it's fun! It also gives you the perfect excuse to go to outdoor clothing stores and try on the array of down jackets on offer. When you find a jacket you like in your budget, go for it — they are superb.

It is a lovely thing to swim in the rain, the surface of the water softened, broken by the raindrops … seeing the tiny splashes each time you turn and breathe … feeling the cool rain on your arms as you take each stroke.

THE
SWIMS

Looking north towards the round tower at Portrane, Donabate, north County Dublin

1

County Dublin

Donabate

Paddle through the shallows, the water lapping around your ankles as you pick up and examine tiny shells with sand crunching beneath your toes, sandals swung loosely in hand: such simple pleasure! This could have been any exotic beach, anywhere in the world, save for the sight that greeted us: fiery red hair above freckled skin, bikini clad and wielding a hurling stick, she looked like a modern-day Irish Boudicca.

A girl plays with hurley and sliotar on Donabate beach, north County Dublin

One could not have scripted such an encounter. This quiet beach was the perfect place to hone her skills. Running and laughing, she and her teammate passed the sliotar between them, trying to keep control of a steady volley back and forth, the gentle crack of leather on ash echoing across the strand. Only in Ireland, aye, but here's the rub: neither of the hurling players were Irish. They were, in fact, French!

A public golf course backs onto Donabate and it is through here that a pleasant walk across the fairway on an old green road, still easy to make out as a low-lying grass track, leads onto the long strand. Dotted along the beach there will be little family groups; parents watching children running in and out of the waves, bright picnic blankets a splash of colour against the pale sand. The huge strand runs for miles between the Rogerstown Estuary to the north and Broadmeadow to the south, both of which are designated Special Areas of Conservation and are superb locations for birdwatching. There is plenty of room here to get well away from the crowds and at only 19km from Dublin city it is very easy to get to.

Nearby Newbridge Demesne is a public park on 370 acres of eighteenth-century parkland, with woods, lawns and wildflower meadows. The mansion, Newbridge House, featured in the 1965 film *The Spy Who Came in from the Cold*, starring Richard Burton.

AT A GLANCE

POPULAR | FAMILY FRIENDLY | SURFING AND KAYAKING

A long and popular strand, Donabate is lifeguarded during the summer months, there are a café and hotel nearby. Walk further south along the beach beside the golf course for less busy areas. 19km north-east of Dublin, Donabate is served by both train and bus routes from Dublin.

BY CAR: from the M1, exit at junction 4, signposted for Donabate. Take the R126 past Newbridge Demesne to Donabate town centre, then turn right onto New Road, heading towards the golf club. There is parking either beside the Waterside House, which is a popular stretch of the beach, or take another right and park on the road beside the links golf course. A public right of way is signed to the beach.

Grid ref: O 25442 49444

Howth, with Ireland's Eye in the background

2

County Dublin

Howth

Only ten minutes north-east of Dublin city centre (thirty minutes on the DART), Howth is a haven for seafood lovers. Howth Market (open weekends and bank holiday Mondays) is beside the DART station and sells crafts, jewellery, antiques and organic foods. From the harbour, there are four walking-route options with coloured arrows to guide you. The cliff path affords spectacular views of Dublin Bay and Ireland's Eye.

On the first weekend of summer a festival vibe sweeps along the coastal path from Howth as hosts of teenagers in swimsuits and shorts flock alongside tourists and walkers. They sweep up past the clifftop shop, towels slung over their shoulders. The pier is now out of bounds – swimmers will be fined if they jump from it – so instead they have reclaimed an old diving haunt a short way along the craggy coastline.

They soon turn left off the trail and drop down a rough, beaten track, making their way to a vertiginous staircase, with no railings. The steps span a cavernous drop to the rocks below and lead to the outcrop where the concrete plinths for old diving boards still remain. The water is deep and clear, a deep, natural diving pit.

Squealing at the chill as they plunge in and swim the few metres to a large islet with the diving platforms, teenagers scramble lithely up the cliff, socks the only protection for bare feet on the barnacle-encrusted stone. The audience shouts encouragement from high above as a wetsuited young man ventures to the highest plinth. He steps to the edge, clenches his fists then backs away, repeatedly going through this performance. The spectators are getting restless and shout, 'Go on, do it! It's not that high.'

It is only when one stands level with the board that one can appreciate the height. The lower board is perhaps 5 metres above the sea, the higher plinth close to 10 metres. There's a lot of time on the way down from 10 metres to realise that you just might have made a mistake.

Four young men line up on the cliff on the other side of the diving pit and one after the other they leap. The sharp smack as their canvas shoes hit the water

Youths jumping from rocks at Howth

The temporary (summer) diving board at Howth

echoes around; their whoops of delight carry up to the crowd. They swim across to a small rock in the middle of the cove and rest in the sun, a *Great Gatsby*-like vision of the seemingly endless summer.

As their confidence grows, the younger boys push themselves to more daring dives, somersaults, spurred on by the crowd and adrenaline. The girls soon join them, somewhat tentatively, before a few begin to brave the higher rocks and board. Soon it is time for us to move on and we leave the rock, as the sun starts to slip down in the sky and we retrace our steps to the harbour and make for home.

AT A GLANCE

JUMPING WITH CARE | SCENIC WALK | GOOD FOOD

On Howth Head, walk the various trails or explore the several hidden coves off the cliff path where one can jump and dive into deep clear waters not far from the harbour and vibrant village. Take the cliff path from the DART station following the purple arrows to the promenade along the harbour. At the end of the prom turn right onto Balscadden Road and climb to Kilrock car park, where you join the path. As the trail climbs higher, look out for a narrow track down to the cove. Push through long grass and bracken until, at a sharp left turn, the rocks and diving plinths can be seen below. Continue down to the staircase and to the rocks, where you can leave your clothes, before swimming just a few metres to the high rock with the diving board and plinths.

BY PUBLIC TRANSPORT: take the DART to Howth or 31A bus from the city centre.

BY BOAT: from Dun Laoghaire, south Dublin, Dublin Bay Cruises sail to Howth.

Grid ref: O 29864 39032

Swimmers at Bull Island, with the Poolbeg chimneys in the background

3

Bull Island

Bull Island on Dublin city's north side continues to grow as the tide deposits sand and silt, forming miles of sandy beach, dunes, mudflats, grasslands and marsh. The island became Ireland's first official bird sanctuary in the 1930s. Swim along the promenade facing Dublin Port and the great Poolbeg chimneys, a well-known landmark. Created 200 years ago this sandspit was formed with the construction of the North Bull Wall. Currently it is 5km long and 1km wide. Just a short trip along the Coast Road between Howth and Dublin, in 1981 it achieved UNESCO Biosphere Reserve status.

Changing areas at Bull Island, looking at the north beach, Dublin

Crossing the single-lane Wooden Bridge onto the island you begin to feel a vitality: this place has a holiday air, swimmers come here regularly and the rows of steps along the sea wall facing the port provide easy access to the water. Along this promenade several bathing shelters have stood the test of time. There are separate areas for women and men, with a mixed bathing area further along, but the rules are not strictly adhered to. Dublin swimmers of all types frequent this pretty island. Here you might share stories with pensioners who have swum every day in life or a marathon swimmer in earnest training for their next big goal, all united in their love of the sea. It is best to swim here facing the port, although the beach appeals to surfers and kitesurfers. Enjoy the walk along the seafront and, at the north of the island you are more likely to find a quiet place to swim.

The island is popular with birdwatchers. You may be lucky enough to spot short-eared owl, snow bunting or even hear a cuckoo. Look out for Irish hare in the dunes.

AT A GLANCE
SCENIC WALK | CITY SWIMMING | EASY FOR KIDS | POPULAR

Swimmers are well catered for on the south end of the island with ladies, men's and mixed changing shelters dotted along the promenade from the Wooden Bridge and banks of steps leading down into the shallow water. Swim at mid to high tide (at low tide you will be walking back across the sand flats). Public toilets are beside the visitor centre and there is car parking on the beach. It is a popular spot with walkers, cyclists, swimmers and kite-surfers.

BY PUBLIC TRANSPORT: take the DART northbound to Raheny station from where a twenty-minute walk down Watermill Road will bring you to Causeway Road to the centre of the island at St Anne's Golf Club and on to the beach.

BY CAR OR BICYCLE: take the Clontarf Road between Dublin and Howth. The Wooden Bridge at Clontarf, close to the port, leads to the prom where most would swim.

Grid ref: O 21423 35739

Above: Changing areas at Bull Island

Left: Getting ready to take the plunge at Bull Island, Dublin

View from the Great South Wall east towards Dublin city

4

County Dublin

Great South Wall

Right in the centre of Dublin Bay and accessed through the docks, the Great South Wall reaches out into Dublin Bay. Halfway along this lengthy jetty you will find the Half Moon Swimming and Waterpolo Club. The whitewashed building provides shelter for swimmers who enjoy the fabulous views back towards the port dominated by the tall Poolbeg chimneys.

The club, founded in 1898 as Poolbeg Bathers' Association, later changed its name to Half Moon Swimming Club. What is now their clubhouse was once a gun battery, the gun turret mounted in a half-moon shape, giving the bay its name. The white-painted buildings are about halfway along the Bull Wall with a changing area and low benches facing the slipway. This becomes a suntrap where, sheltered from the wind, one can sit and enjoy an after-swim hot cuppa and watch the great ships sailing in and out of the port.

To the south, Sandymount Strand attracts walkers and kitesurfers. This was once known as the Waxies' Dargle: in the nineteenth century, the rich would picnic at the Dargle River in the Wicklow Mountains; however, Sandymount was as much as the poor could hope for and it became known as the Waxies' (cobblers') Dargle.

In the early 1700s construction started on what was to become the Great South Wall, built because of the troublesome sandbars that obstructed the entrance to Dublin Port. First thick oak piles were driven into the clay and anchored with baskets of gravel. A stone wall linking the piles to the quay was completed several decades later and soon the walls were strengthened with massive granite blocks from Dalkey Quarry. By 1795 the wall was completed, 10 metres thick at the base and 8 metres at the top. At the end of the Great

Poolbeg Lighthouse at the end of the Great South Wall

At the Half Moon Swimming Club changing area

South Wall is Poolbeg Lighthouse, painted red to indicate port side for ships entering Dublin Bay (the North Bull Lighthouse, 330 metres north, is painted green to indicate starboard).

In 2008 the Great South Wall was the venue for one of Spencer Tunick's en masse nude photo shoots, involving more than 2,000 people lined up along the wall.

Sandymount, 3km south-east of Dublin city centre, is a huge strand which featured in Joyce's *Ulysses*. At low tide the sand stretches out as far as the eye can see. This strand can be dangerous so watch the tides as they can come in fast behind you, cutting you off. Popular with walkers and kitesurfers, it is a great entryway to the Great South Wall and the village has plenty of cafés and pubs in which to end the day.

AT A GLANCE

SCENIC WALK | GOOD FOOD & PUBS | SHALLOW BAY | CITY SWIMMING | ICONIC VIEWS AND SWIM

Take a swim from the slipway on the south side of the wall while great ships cruise in and out of the docks on the north side. Look up to the iconic Poolbeg chimneys, and warm up with a walk to Poolbeg Lighthouse. At the far end of the wall, there are great views back to the city. Best to swim here at mid to high tide. The rocks at the end of the slipway and bottom of the ladder make it unsafe for jumping and diving.

BY CAR: from the north side of Dublin city, head for the signposted Eastlink toll bridge in the Docklands. Shortly after the tollbooths, at the large roundabout take the opposite exit, South Bank Road, after approximately 200 metres turn left onto White Bank Road. This road takes a sharp left and becomes Pigeon House Road. Continue through the docks for approximately 1km, then turn right towards the shoreline. Follow Shelly Banks Road which zigzags around the power station, you can either park at the car park or continue along to park on the roadside near the South Wall. There is a limited amount of parking a few hundred metres along the wall itself.

From Dublin's south side, the signs to the Eastlink will bring you to the roundabout, before crossing the Liffey. Take the South Bank Road and follow above directions.

ON FOOT: about an hour's walk from the city centre or take the Red Line of the Luas tram service, alighting at Point Village. From here, walk through the Docklands and alongside the beach to the Wall.

Grid refs:
Great South Wall: O 22359 33860
Sandymount: O 19129 33062

An artist sketches the Forty Foot at Sandycove, south Dublin

5

Forty Foot, Sandycove

The beauty of Dublin City swimming is its accessibility via public transport, with DART stations near each site. This conveys the impression of the city as a series of villages that have been amalgamated into the metropolis as it has grown, although each village has managed to keep its own identity. Dublin is a vibrant, living thing and at its heart a pulse of cyclists, runners, walkers and swimmers all keep it thriving.

The Martello tower above the rocky cove features in the opening scene of James Joyce's epic novel *Ulysses* and now houses the James Joyce Museum. For 250 years Dubliners have been leaping into the sea here. Joyce himself was a keen participant, and in *Ulysses* refers to 'the sea, the snotgreen sea, the scrotumtightening sea'. This promontory on the southern tip of Dublin Bay was, until the 1970s, exclusively a gentlemen's bathing area and, because it was isolated and men only, became popular with nudists. The nearby Sandycove Harbour was the ladies' and children's bathing area. Since female-rights activists plunged in, in the 1970s, the Forty Foot has welcomed all. The sign remains, though: *'Gentlemen's Bathing Place'*.

There is a narrow entrance, which opens out to a changing area. Painted walls block the worst of the offshore breeze and a small lip at the top provides a modicum of shelter on rainy days. Steps lead down into the water with a single handrail to help steady oneself on slippery rocks. At the bottom step, the only thing to do is launch oneself forward and out into this craggy bay.

Although some people dive in from the rocks, it is dangerous. Take heed of the warning signs. Sandycove Bathers' Association help with the upkeep of the area which is funded by voluntary donations. It is a short walk from the Forty Foot to Sandycove Harbour.

AT A GLANCE

JUMPING WITH CARE | CITY SWIMMING | EASY ACCESS | PUBLIC TRANSPORT

The Forty Foot is popular with all ages and levels of swimmer and for anyone visiting Dublin it really is a must-see place. A craggy cove with steps and ladders into the water, it has the added bonus of the sheltered Sandycove just a short walk away.

BY PUBLIC TRANSPORT: from Dublin city take the DART to Sandycove/Glasthule. Turn right heading southwards on Glasthule Road. Take the first left, onto Islington Avenue towards the shore, then turn right and walk ten to fifteen minutes along the front. You will see the tiny Sandycove Harbour at the end of the bay. From the harbour there is a narrow path to the Forty Foot and the Martello tower.

BY CAR: follow the signs to Dun Laoghaire, N11 then N31. As you pass through the busy Dun Laoghaire harbour area, the small Sandycove Harbour is visible ahead. Turn down the narrow road at Sandycove, park here and walk the path over a small rise to the Forty Foot.

Grid ref: O 25829 28210

The Vico, south Dublin

County Dublin

The Vico, Dalkey

Dublin city has a great tradition of al fresco swimming: for over 200 years, swimmers have been frequenting the famous Forty Foot at Dun Laoghaire. Further south on the Vico Road, the pretty area of Dalkey boasts a similar bathing area known simply as The Vico. Harder to find than its famous sibling, the Vico lies hidden, nestled along the cliff edge between Dalkey and Killiney beach. Swimwear is optional here.

The Vico, looking towards the Wicklow Mountains, south Dublin

Thirty minutes from the city on the southbound DART to Dalkey, Dublin's original seaside resort has a Mediterranean feel and the area is known locally as the Bay of Naples. As you climb away from Dalkey along the Vico Road, a small gap in the seaward wall marks the entrance to the path that first goes across a high-sided footbridge over the railway line and then down towards the shore. From the bridge there are fantastic views of Dalkey Island on the left and Killiney Bay to the right. As the path zigzags further down the steep hillside, you get your first view of the Vico bathing area.

Surfboards line the railings and the whitewashed shelter built into the rocks stands out against the grey.

Handwritten on a board the words 'swimwear optional' and a white-painted changing shelter above the ladders welcome you in. Steep steps with handrails lead down over the rocks to the water. To one side a small seawater pool mirrors the sky, a sharp contrast to the choppy ocean. Swim from here toward the White Rocks bathing area (naturist until noon) and gaze up at the stunning houses perched on the cliff above.

Dipping a toe into the bathing pool at the Vico, Dublin

AT A GLANCE

NATURIST & SKINNY-DIPPING | CITY SWIMMING | ROCKS AND ROCK POOL

Swimwear is optional at this hidden bathing spot. Steps and ladders lead down into the deep water and you can mull about close to the Vico or strike out across the bay towards White Rocks and Killiney Beach. One of the last bastions of 'au naturel' swimming, the Vico is quieter and harder to find than the popular Forty Foot but well worth the effort.

White Rocks Bathing Area —a grassy picnic area at the roadside leads down to a path to the beach. Naturist until noon.

BY CAR: from Killiney take the Victoria and then Vico Road past Victoria Park. At White Rocks Bathing Area there is a lay-by with car parking space. Go on foot from here as there is no parking further along this road. As the road sweeps left and drops down, there is a small gap in the wall on the seaward side. Take this path, across the footbridge and down to The Vico Bathing Area.

Grid refs:
Vico: O 26943 25950
White Rocks: O 26489 25810

7

County Wicklow

Sallymount Naturist Beach, Brittas

Less than an hour's drive south from Dublin, Brittas is one of the best-known beaches in Ireland. It stretches along the east coast of Wicklow, 5km of sand and dunes. While the main beach is very popular with families and has several camping and caravan sites, further south is the little-known naturist beach, Sallymount.

Swimming nude feels great: no suit to chafe the skin, the whole body feels the water and, when getting out, no struggle out of a soaking swimsuit while trying to preserve modesty under a flapping towel. The naturist simply strides out of the water and lets the air and sun do the drying: much more comfortable!

View south on Sallymount, known for its naturism, Brittas Bay, Wicklow

The tide is turning in favour of 'au naturel' swimming and there are now a growing number of people who strip off for charity; the 'Dip in the Nip' in aid of cancer charities encourages hundreds of people to jump into the sea, naked.

Although there are many secluded beaches around Ireland that naturists use, there are, in fact, no officially approved naturist beaches. Public nudity is still somewhat of a taboo in Ireland but attitudes are beginning to thaw, and the Irish Naturist Association, which has been in existence for over fifty years, continues to campaign for official clothing-optional facilities.

In the seventeenth century, the infamous pirate Captain Jack White operated from the cove now known as 'Jack's Hole', smuggling goods from British merchant ships and importing from France, avoiding customs. He had a lucrative business until his accomplice, the sheriff of the Grand Jury, felt that Jack was getting too bold and so had him tried and hanged.

Brittas is a popular family beach and many come here to walk and swim. The water gets deep gradually and at the height of summer the beach can be busy. Walk south of the main beach to find the naturist area where you can swim and sunbathe at ease.

AT A GLANCE

FAMILY FRIENDLY | POPULAR | NATURIST

Brittas is a popular family beach on the east coast of Wicklow, approximately 60km south of Dublin with 5km of sandy beach backed by dunes. The naturist area is a long, sandy beach at the southern end of the main beach.

BY CAR: follow the N11 from Dublin, exiting at the signs for Brittas Bay at Jack White's Cross Roads. Continue on towards Brittas Bay on Cornagower Park for 2.5km to a T-junction. Turn right onto the R750 and travel a further 3.4km to a group of fir trees on the left with a road to the right: park on the roadside here. Opposite this road junction is a small gate marked 'Buckrooney'. Walk through the gate and follow the path through the sand dunes to the naturist part of the beach.

As there are no officially approved naturist beaches in Ireland swimming or sunbathing nude on a public beach is illegal. The website of the Irish Naturist Association recommends using discretion and common sense to avoid problems and says that no member of the association has ever been prosecuted for naturist activities.

Grid ref: T 28887 79721 (parking at roadside gate)

Naturists relax at Sallymount, Brittas Bay, Wicklow

Looking along the numerous small beaches and coves, from Kilmichael Point, Wexford, north towards Kilmurry Lower in County Wicklow

8

Kilmichael Point and Kilpatrick

Kilmichael Point is just south of the Wicklow/Wexford border, a mere 6.5km from Arklow and the popular Clogga Strand. From Kilmichael Point there is a series of tiny sandy beaches just perfect to clamber down to and find your own private swimming cove. One can also walk a grass track along the dunes south, all the way to the sweeping strand of Kilpatrick Beach.

View from Kilmichael sand dunes towards Kilpatrick Beach, Wexford

Following the signs from Arklow for Kilmichael Point brings you finally down a narrow lane to a dead end with a small turning circle and a pretty terrace of stone cottages. This row of now refurbished homes were originally built as a coastguard station in the mid 1800s. There are several small sandy coves here, each bordered by a flank of rocks, which you can scramble down to in front of the terrace. The water is shallow and it is nice to swim at low tide or paddle around the rocks from one bay into the next. Spend a quiet afternoon here enjoying the small coves that stretch both to the north and the south of Kilmichael Point.

On the other side of the row of cottages a rough grass track goes south along the coast through the Kilpatrick sand dunes. The remains of several buildings are dotted across the fields, perhaps farm dwellings long abandoned. A small, square building, now deserted, seems to have been a lookout sometime in the past with a wide opening facing the sea. As you head south through Kilpatrick each rise leads to a new cove enticing you to explore further.

After fifteen to twenty minutes' walking, you come to a great swathe of sand sweeping across the grass into the centre of the fields – odd, like a desert in the middle of an oasis. It looks as if the beach is invading the fields behind. Now you have reached Kilpatrick Beach. From this approach, you will find a quiet corner. Kilpatrick is known for its interesting and rare seashells.

AT A GLANCE

SECLUDED | FAMILY FRIENDLY | SCENIC WALK

A series of small sandy coves that can be climbed down to, or take a walk along the coast path south to the sand dunes of the popular Kilpatrick Beach. A small turning circle provides some parking space in front of pretty stone cottages, originally a coastguard station built c. 1847 and now residential.

BY CAR: from Dublin take the M11 past Bray and Wicklow town to Arklow. Exit at Junction 21 to follow the R772 from Arklow and Clogga towards Castletown. Before reaching Castletown take a left turn, signposted for Kilmichael Point, which leads to a terrace of three stone cottages.

Grid ref:
Kilmichael Point: T 25509 66598
Kilpatrick Beach & Dunes: T 2519 65982

Second World War lookout post at Kilmichael Point, Wexford

Baginbun Head, Wexford

9

County Wexford

Baginbun Head, Hook Peninsula

About 2km south of Fethard-on-Sea and 8km north-east of Hook Head Light-house, Baginbun is a secluded and picturesque bay with a distinctive Martello tower dating from the Napoleonic wars. It is hard to resist visting a place with

the Hobbit-esque name of Baginbun. One imagines a beautiful, hidden and exciting place, and Baginbun does not disappoint. The approach is convoluted and after a while you think you have missed the beach completely. The signs will, however, bring you close to the Martello tower on the promontory. The beach lies below.

Baginbun on the Hook Peninsula has been a military stronghold since 500 BC. The Martello tower is a remnant from the Napoleonic Wars, and now the beach is a place for families to come to picnic and play.

From the roadside parking there is a bird's-eye view of the bay, the steep sandy cliffs dropping down to a fine golden strand and a modern house looking out past the remains of the tower to sea. Follow the track alongside a wooden fence to the steep concrete path down to the beach. The high cliffs form a suntrap and the sand is warm on your feet as the sun beams down.

This tranquil bay holds a dark history: it is the site of the second Anglo-Norman invasion in 1170. A small band of around eighty men came, led by the cunning Raymond le Gros who chose Baginbun for its ancient Irish fort, which he planned to use as a defence camp before attacking Waterford. Needing supplies, he sent his men to raid for cattle and they brought a herd back to the fort. It is estimated between 1,000 and 3,000 angry Waterford men marched to Baginbun, confident of beating the small army they

Martello tower on Baginbun Head

met there. Raymond, however, ordered his troops to attack, then retreat in feigned panic. As the Waterford men charged after them, Raymond loosed the cattle in a stampede, scattering his attackers, killing many and capturing more. One struggles to imagine such a bloody battle on this picturesque shore.

Looking west from Baginbun Head, Wexford

AT A GLANCE

FAMILY FRIENDLY | POPULAR

Shallow and safe for swimming, this beach is less populated than the main one at Fethard-on-Sea. To get to the beach, there is a short walk along the top of the sand cliffs, then a steep path down.

BY CAR: from Wellingtonbridge south-east of Wexford town, take the R733 towards Arthurstown, then the R734 to Fethard and follow the signs to Baginbun Head. Park at the top of the cliffs and follow the rough track above the beach to the steep path down.

Grid ref: S 79909 03169

View west over Dollar Bay and the path to the beach, Wexford

10

County Wexford

Dollar Bay, Hook Peninsula

The Ring of Hook coastal drive takes you past crumbling ruins and the Templar Inn restaurant, famed for its seafood, to many small beaches, including Baginbun Head, with its Martello tower, and Dollar and Booley Bays. Approximately 8km north of Hook Lighthouse, Dollar Bay is signed as a sea-fishing beach. Quiet with high, sandy cliffs that curve around to several rocky outcrops, which give shelter from the prevailing winds, this secluded beach is good for swimming at either high or low tide.

Above and facing page: Booley Bay, Wexford

Dollar Bay was named for the hoard of Spanish milled gold that was buried here by mutineers in November 1765. The brutal tale tells of how four crewmen of the Earl of Sandwich attacked and killed their shipmates and captain, all save the cabin boy. They flooded the ship and watched it capsize, ignoring the poor cabin boy's cries as he scrambled up the mast. The robbers rowed away, coming ashore at Dollar Bay. Only able to carry one bag of gold between them, they buried the rest of the sacks in the sand. As they made their getaway towards Dublin, the sinking ship drifted to shore at Sheep Island with the cabin boy still clinging to the wreck. Rescued, he told his story and the search began for the mutineers. News of four men spending Spanish gold spread quickly and they were soon caught and hanged for their crimes.

No need to rush here with a shovel, though: the gold was all recovered and the beach is now a place where you can swim in tranquillity, with no trace of the underhand dealings of the past.

The neighbouring beach at Booley Bay is similarly sheltered, attracts just a few visitors and has the benefit of a large, flat grassy area, perfect for wild camping above the high-water mark. Check out the nearby Templar Inn for great seafood on the way to Dollar and Booley. Further along this coast road is Duncannon, a well-liked family beach, with a lifeguard during the summer and popular with kitesurfers.

AT A GLANCE

FAMILY FRIENDLY | SECLUDED | GOOD FOOD | BEACH CAMPING | SHRIMPING & SNORKELLING

A sheltered, sandy beach, which shelves gently to beautiful swimming in a shallow cove.

BY CAR: from Wexford city take the N25 towards Rosslare. Turn right onto the R733 through Wellingtonbridge and on towards Arthurstown. Turn left onto R734 towards Fethard-on-Sea and the Ring of Hook coastal drive.

Following the Ring of Hook drive take the road past the Templar Inn. After a few kilometres there is a left turn signed for Dollar Bay Beach Fishing. Park along the lane and walk the steep gravel path down to the beach.

Grid refs:
Dollar Bay: S 75068 05570
Booley Bay: S 75009 06020

Swimming at Hook Head Lighthouse, Wexford

11

County Wexford

Hook Head Lighthouse

Close to the border of counties Wexford and Waterford is the long finger of Hook Peninsula, pointing south-west into St George's Channel. Hook is said to have been the origin of the saying 'by hook or by crook' back in 1170. On his way to capture Waterford, the Earl of Pembroke reputedly instructed his men to land at either Hook, on the Wexford side of the estuary, or by the village of Crooke in Waterford.

One of the deep channels at Hook Head

At the very tip of this narrow peninsula, Ireland's oldest working lighthouse welcomes visitors and the guided tour is popular. Stroll around the grounds and admire the views. To the front of the lighthouse, climb down the rocks and step across a thin crack through which the water washing deep beneath can be glimpsed. Soon you will see the large rock pool that provides this dramatic swim. Beneath the lighthouse a stone wall drops down into a deep, narrow channel, opposite which the rocks are stepped down to the water's edge. The crashing waves are broken before they enter the pool and disperse into sea foam, the texture of bubble bath. Care should be taken getting in as the seaweed covering the rocks can be very slippery but on reaching the deep water closer to the lighthouse you can enjoy short laps along this channel.

Hook Head has had a beacon here since medieval times and the current lighthouse is over 800 years old, still working although now automated. It is the oldest working lighthouse in Ireland and one of the oldest in Europe. Popular with visitors one can tour all year round. There is a good café and local artists sell their work here.

AT A GLANCE

STRONG SWIMMERS ONLY | TIDAL ROCK POOL | POPULAR
TOURIST SITE | GOOD FOOD

Swim at Ireland's oldest working lighthouse in this large natural
pool at mid to high tide. Be prepared to have an audience but
you can get some great photos! For strong swimmers only, and
only in calm conditions. Take care getting in as the rocks are
covered in barnacles and seaweed. There is a thick covering of
kelp at low tide.

BY CAR: Hook Head is on the R734, 50km from Wexford city and
29km from Waterford via the Passage East ferry. Take the scenic
Ring of Hook through Fethard-on-Sea and drive to the tip of the
peninsula to the lighthouse.

Grid ref: X 73385 97384

The south-facing channel at Hook Head Lighthouse

Hook Head lighthouse

12

County Waterford

Guillamene and Newtown Coves, Tramore

Diving boards at Newtown and Guillamene, County Waterford

Despite the men-only sign, all visitors are welcomed at Guillamene and it is a must-swim at the gateway to the Copper Coast. The community of swimmers has grown here over seventy years or so and, while children and teens throw themselves from the diving board and casual swimmers enjoy the deep waters, adventure swimmers can tour the coast heading west, away from Tramore, to explore a remarkable cave swim.

Tramore is a bustling holiday town with a long strand stretching 5km where horse races are held and surf schools abound. The promenade bustles with amusements, cafés and a funfair and the Surf Lifesaving National Centre runs various courses. Behind the sandspit of the main strand is

The men-only sign at Guillamene

Newtown and Guillamene Swimming Cove, County Waterford

a tidal lagoon known as the Back Strand, where wild fowl abound and, if you walk here at twilight, you may be lucky enough to see an owl hunting.

Just 3km from the busy promenade at Tramore, the coves of Newtown and Guillamene have been popular for swimming for over seventy years. As one follows the signs for the swimming club, the road sweeps down to a wooded area. A track leads into the trees from the roadside footpath: this is the entrance to the ladies' bathing area of Newtown Cove. Continue on to the ample car park at Guillamene. A small white toilet block beside the tended lawn leads to the concrete steps going down to the bathing area and diving board. At the other side of the car park a second set of stairs leads to Newtown Cove and you can choose which you prefer to swim at. This first set of steps leads down to concreted platforms. 'No Fishing' signs painted on the ground designate the swimmers' area. Those wanting to fish have plenty of sites around the rocks to the right of the cove, so if you plan to swim this direction just give them a wide berth.

The board at Guillamene is approximately 3 metres above the water (depending on the tide) and ladders to climb out are dotted around the cove.

Approximately 1km along the coast, towards the mouth of the bay and under the Metal Man statue and pillar, there is a large cave. Deep and black and reverberating with the low boom of the moving water it feels threatening to swim into but one can indeed swim right through and out the far side. (Local man Donal Buckley (http://loneswimmer.com) might be kind enough to give you a guided tour.) It is an exposed and advanced swim from Guillamene to the cave and so suitable for strong swimmers only. From Guillamene Cove turn right and follow the coastline for approximately 1km. High on the cliff above is the statue of the Metal Man pointing out to sea. Watch out for the mouth of the cave between two outcrops of jagged rock. The opening is a tall, narrow arch leading into inky depths. Listen to the echoes as you stroke your way inside and your eyes adjust to the darkness. The water gets shallow as you clamber over the stones onto this subterranean shore. To the left, light seeps in through a low arch and here you can swim back out into the daylight world. You are now at the western end of Tramore Bay. To return to Guillamene, keep the shore on your left as you retrace your strokes, passing the large opening where you first entered the cave.

When you return to the cove and dress, you may want to buy an ice cream from the quirky Ice Cream Tractor at the car park. There is a small toilet block and a grassy area for picnicking.

The Newtown and Guillamene Swimming Club maintains the area and promotes it, ensuring the diving board and steps to access the water are kept clean and litter free.

AT A GLANCE

FAMILY FRIENDLY | SWIMMING, JUMPING, DIVING | ADVENTURE SWIM | CAVE SWIM

The twin coves of Guillamene and Newtown are 3km from Tramore promenade, popular swimming holes with a thriving swim community. Swim the exposed kilometre along the coast to the large cave under the Metal Man.

BY CAR: from Waterford city take the N25 south-west towards Dungarvan and Cork, then the R682 to Tramore. From here, take the coast road west and follow the signs for Newtown and Guillamene. Turn left to Newtown Caravan and Camping, then left again to Newtown and Guillamene Swimming Club. There is a path through the woods down to Newtown Cove. Park on the roadside or continue around to the large car park at Guillamene where you can access either cove via steep steps.

Grid refs:
Guillamene: X 57138 99404
Tramore: S 58405 01168
Newtown Cove: X 57115 99320
Metal Man: X 56787 98602

13

County Waterford

Ballydowane, Copper Coast

With jagged rocks and promontories that shelter each bay from the next, the best way to explore the Copper Coast is by car or bicycle. This rugged coastline has 25km of scalloped beaches and bays, named after the nineteenth-century copper mines that have helped to form the many sea arches and caves. Pretty villages and thatched cottages line the route of the South-east Coastal Drive, passing one cove after another.

Above and facing page: Ballydowane beach on County Waterford's Copper Coast

This is a series of sand and gravel beaches, the cliffs ranging in colour from grey, through red to purples, and pockmarked with the trademark holes and caves left behind from the mining industry that gave the region its name. Despite the rough and sometimes brutal landscape, the water is warm and many of the coves shelve gently, providing lovely swimming.

At Ballydowane, between Bunmahon and Stradbally, the entrance to the beach is not inspiring: a narrow laneway leads to a basic parking circle which then peters out into a short ramp onto the beach. Two great stacks on either side of this ramp hide the true expanse of the bay. It is only when you step out from their shadow that the view opens out and your breath is taken away by the rugged landscape. With fine grey sand, dotted with bright yellow and white seashells, stepping onto this beach is to enter another world. The red-and-purple cliffs hold inside them a Jurassic scene, and

huge sea stacks jut out of the water like a mythical sea creature. Here the rocks are home to a wealth of fish if you want to try to catch your supper or simply enjoy some interesting snorkelling in the shallow water. The deep waters are only suitable for strong swimmers due to the tides and currents here. Always swim parallel to shore and within your depth unless you have an accompanying kayak.

While swimming across the bay, look up at the great walls enclosing the beach. The layers of crumbling rock have been marked by each winter storm, changing the shape of the cliffs as they are battered by wind and waves. To the far left of the bay the prominent shark-fin-shaped stack is fun to investigate. Watch out as you swim around it and see if you can find the narrow entrance to the cave underneath.

AT A GLANCE

STRONG SWIMMERS | ROCK POOLS

The sandy beach of Ballydowane Bay is surrounded by impressive red-brown cliffs and has rock pools to explore, good swimming across the bay and snorkelling around the sea stacks. The water gradually gets deeper. There are some currents here, which make it suitable for strong swimmers only.

BY CAR: from Dungarvan, west of Waterford city, take the R675 towards Tramore. Follow this road, and take the right-hand turn for Stradbally. As you come into Stradbally, take the right-hand turn signposted for Ballyvooney. After a few kilometres, take another right-hand turn, this time signposted for Ballydowane Bay.

Grid ref: X 40765 97906

14

County Cork

Simon's Cove, Courtmacsherry

There are two coves for the price of one here at the hidden Simon's Cove: in the main cove, smooth giant rocks form beautiful carved shapes. The pebble beach quickly gets to a nice depth for swimming and the high rocks create a cove that is interesting to explore, both for swimming and climbing its walls. Across the rocks a second small shale beach tucked beneath the rock pavement is perfect for jumping at high water.

Few swimmers know about this hidden bay at the end of the single-track road from Courtmacsherry. Fewer still take the walk along the shoreline trail to the right, squeezing past the front of the house and down the narrow path onto the tessellated

Swimmers venture out of Simon's Cove, Courtmacsherry, County Cork

rocks along the shore. A few hundred metres leads to a pavement of flat black rock, which abruptly drops away to reveal a curve of shale forming a tiny beach. A narrow channel from the sea between the high black rocks fills this tiny bay. As you look from above, the rock pool seems to open out like a fan as the water flows in in the rising tide.

This womb-like pool is sheltered by the high rocks around and, while children play safely contained, strong swimmers may slip out through this funnel between the rocks and swim along the coast in the open sea. At high water this is a great place for jumping and diving and children will enjoy scouring the rock pools in search of sea urchin and crabs. Return to the main cove where there is a high path on the left side of the beach which leads around the cliffs to Butlerstown Cove, a lovely walk on good weather days.

This is a lovely place to come on the opposite side of Clonakilty Bay, away from the popular Inchydoney strand.

AT A GLANCE

FAMILY FRIENDLY | JUMPING WITH CARE

A small cove 6km south of Clonakilty with smooth rocks to scramble over plus a second rock pool just a short walk around the shore where at high water one can jump from the rocks.

BY CAR: from Cork city take the N25, then the N71 south-west to Clonakilty. Head east from Clonakilty and take a right onto the Old Timoleague Road. Follow the shore past Deasy's Seafood Restaurant and Bar; the road goes left, away from the coast. Turn right at the next crossroads. Continue along this road looking out for the sign to Simon's Cove. This single-track road runs for 1.5km down to the cove where there is a small turning circle beside a modern stone house.

Grid refs:
Simon's Cove: W 42934 38221
Rock pool: W 42809 38164

Swimmers preparing for their daily
dip at Simon's Cove, Courtmacsherry,
County Cork

County Cork

Lough Hyne

Underwater in Lough Hyne, County Cork

Lough Hyne, County Cork

Barlogue Creek, leading to The Rapids

Until 4,000 years ago Lough Hyne was a freshwater lake, then rising sea levels swamped it with seawater. The tide flows in to fill the lough twice a day through the narrow channel on the north-eastern corner of the lake, thus creating a warm lake of oxygenated seawater which sustains a huge variety of marine plants, animals and fish.

Sitting in a fold of hills 5km south of the market town of Skibbereen, this marine lake has a unique ecosystem and is home to a wide range of plants and animals. At less than 1km long and 0.75km wide, the lough is connected to the Atlantic Ocean by a narrow channel known as The Rapids. As the tide ebbs and flows the lake is replenished and this serves to maintain its varied sea life. This is Ireland's first Marine Nature Reserve. Since 1886, scientists have carried out research in experimental ecology, looking into the factors governing the distribution of marine plants and animals, making Lough Hyne one of the most studied marine sites in Europe. Check out Skibbereen Heritage Centre, which has an audio-video documentary on the area's history and folklore and there are panels depicting the more common species to be found in the lake.

At the height of the flood, the tide rushes in through the rapids at speeds up to 16km/h, creating the fast-flowing water which kayakers regularly paddle out into. Some swimmers bring out inflatables to shoot the wild waters.

The little island outcrop on the shore facing the grand house is the preferred entry point for most swimmers. Here you can wade in down a short, wide slipway into the clear water.

This is home to the Lough Hyne Lappers, a group of open-water swimmers who boast amongst their numbers the first man to complete the Oceans Seven (a challenge to swim seven of the major sea crossings, including the English and North channels). Lough Hyne is not just for these hardy marathon swimmers, though, and you might just as soon meet grandparents introducing their grandchildren to the water.

Swim out and around Castle Island in the centre of the lake with the ancient ruins of Cloghan Castle, once the O'Driscoll stronghold. According to local legend, King Labhra Loinseach who lived here had the ears of a donkey! The swim out around the island and back is approximately 1,500 metres, the rapids are to be found past the left of Castle Island in the north-eastern corner of the lake. As the crow flies it is almost a kilometre from the entry point to the rapids behind Castle Island.

The lake is surrounded by woodland and has a magical air. A nature trail takes you on a steep walk up through the woods of Knockomagh Hill overlooking the lough. There are too loops, one north and one south, and from the south loop one can also reach the summit, from where there are grandstand views of west Cork, Lough Hyne and out to the Atlantic Ocean. This is approximately an hour's walk.

AT A GLANCE

FAMILY FRIENDLY | SCENIC WALK | SNORKELLING | BOATS OR CANOES | SWIM TO THE ISLAND

Swim in the clear briny waters of this sea lough, take a long swim around Castle Island or play in the strong-moving flow of The Rapids during the ebb and flow tides. With its abundant sea life it is well worth bringing a mask and snorkel for your visit here. There is room to park near this slipway and a picnic area.

BY CAR: from Skibbereen in west Cork take the R595 toward Baltimore and after a few kilometres, take a left turn, signed to Lough Hyne. This leads down to the parking at the edge of the lake. Turn left and drive along the lakeshore to the outcrop and slipway.

Grid ref: W 09528 28872

Glanmore Lake, Beara Peninsula

Slip into tranquil waters from the tree-shaded lake shore to swim through the reflections of the towering Caha Mountains, weave around tiny rock islands with trees perched atop, growing in impossibly little soil. Climb onto the larger island, built as a crannóg. Its stone hermitage is now overgrown but this little building calls out to be explored.

Seen at its best looking down from the Healy Pass, Glanmore is one of the nicest lake swims on the peninsula. Set at the base of the steep slopes of Lackabane Mountain, trees reaching up to the sky, it could be deep in the Canadian wilderness. On the near side the road follows the lakeshore. Quiet and surrounded by trees, there is ample opportunity to swim and plenty of places for skinny-dipping.

On a calm day the lake waters act as a mirror, reflecting the Caha Mountains and broken only by the occasional trout jumping, spreading concentric rings out across the surface. Silence pervades the glen and it feels like a thousand miles from civilisation. Slipping into the lake you realise it is alive with tiny insects flitting along the surface: it is these the trout are jumping for. They move away as you pass. You may want

Below and previous spread: Reflective Glanmore Lake, looking towards the Ring of Kerry, Beara Peninsula, County Kerry

to swim out to one of the many little islets dotted through the lake, making your way from one to the next. Check out the largest, a crannóg, on which there is an almost overgrown stone building that once housed the sheltering animals.

Walkers will enjoy spending a few days exploring the area and there is a range of degrees of difficulty, from rambling the lakeshore to venturing deeper into the Caha Mountains. Check out Pedals and Boots Café near Lauragh, which uses local ingredients and stocks artisan products from the Beara Peninsula.

Josie's Restaurant provides good meals and bed and breakfast accommodation or try Glanmore Lake Hostel, an old schoolhouse at the foot of the Healy Pass on the south-west shore of the lake. Several cottages in the area are available for hire.

The Beara Peninsula lies between the Kenmare River to the north and Bantry Bay to the south; the Caha and Slieve Miskish Mountains run down its centre. The northern part of the peninsula is in county Kerry and the rest in County Cork. Glanmore Lake is in Kerry, close to the county border. It has an abundance of walking routes, both short and long distance, such as the Beara Way, which is based on part of the march of O'Sullivan Beare in 1603.

AT A GLANCE

SCENIC WALK | SECLUDED | SKINNY-DIPPING | ISLANDS | NEARBY HOSTEL AND RESTAURANT

The pristine Glanmore Lake has many tiny rock islands, a crannóg and trout. Across from the lake the sheer slopes of Lackabane Mountain rise up, pine trees stretching towards the sun.

BY CAR OR BICYCLE: from Kenmare in County Kerry, cross the bridge over the Kenmare River and turn right onto the R571. This junction has an astounding twenty signs so don't even try to read them! Follow the shores along the river passing several loughs (which are easily accessed for a swim from the road, but what would be the fun in that?). Enjoy the scenery as you wind along the riverbank for 24km to Lauragh.

From Lauragh take the R574 Healy Pass road, past the old pub, An Síbín. Turn left, following the signs for Josie's Lakeview Restaurant. Keep on along this narrow road climbing further into the mountains. Every so often a small pointer for Josie's affirms you are not lost. As you drop down and pass the entrance to Josie's, the first view of the lake will appear. Drive down to the junction where a second road follows the lakeshore and choose your spot.

Grid ref: V 77391 55706

17

County Cork

Allihies, Beara Peninsula

Viewed from above, the bank of white sand at Ballydonegan Bay on the Beara Peninsula looks as though it has flowed down the hillside. Deep and soft, this strange ore-type sand has been carried down by the small river from the copper mines above Allihies and stands out against the rugged coastline and barren hillside behind. Nearing the tip of the peninsula this beautiful beach seems to be at the end of the world, with sun glinting on wave crests on the shimmering ocean beyond.

Allihies Beach looking towards Garnish Point, Beara Peninsula, County Cork

The village of Allihies stands on the hillside above the rugged splendour of the beach and Ballydonegan Bay. One is drawn to this welcoming little oasis, which hugs the hillside, with its vibrant, painted buildings and a relaxed atmosphere at the end of summer. Dotted around are the remains of the copper-mining industry: stone buildings with curiously shaped chimneys, balanced on impossibly small ridges climbing towards the top of the mountain.

Below, the white beach looks as though the sand has been carried in truckloads to make that impressively deep bank smothering the little bay. The water reaches from pale blue shallows to the deep blue-grey of the ocean and Dursey Island is visible to the west.

To the right of the beach, leading up to the pier, the stark white concrete sea-defence wall is elegant in its simplicity, its stepped formation providing shelter, seating and reflecting the sun's warmth.

The water shelves steeply to a good depth for swimming and several small groups of rocks are scattered along the beach. As you swim, watch for the pinnacles of rocks close to the pier, which are hidden at high tide. You might be swimming in deep water then suddenly come across a small reef, so keep an eye open for these. They make great diving platforms: climb onto one and find yourself standing tall, knees out of the water, then execute your stylish dive back into the deeper water.

Spend the day here, picnicking and swimming below the town. The small river to the left of the strand provides hours of entertainment for children. Take in some of the local walking trails, signposted in Allihies, and finish the day enjoying the last of the evening sunshine sipping a beer outside O'Neill's bar on the main street.

AT A GLANCE

FAMILY FRIENDLY | CAMPING | HOSTELS AND RENTAL ACCOMMODATION | GOOD FOOD |
SCENIC WALKS

The beach at Ballydonegan Bay sits below the brightly painted town of Allihies, a deep swathe of
white sand, stark against the grey-green land and turquoise sea. To the right, the pale concrete
bank of sea defence wall creates a suntrap for beach-goers, its tall steps providing seating close to
the water's edge. There are some strong currents here so stay close to the beach and swim parallel
to shore.

BY CAR: following the Ring of Beara, a 148km driving and cycle route from Kenmare, Allihies is at
the far west of the peninsula. Take the R571 from Kenmare towards Eyeries, then the R575 to
Allihies. The beach lies below the town.

Grid ref: V 57465 44261

Old wooden sea defence at Allihies

18

County Cork

Forge Cove and Amphitheatre, Beara Peninsula

Travelling west along the R571, the Ring of Beara gives unparalleled views of Coulagh Bay to the north and the Miskish Mountains to the south. Along this road on the approach to Cod's Head on the north-west tip of the peninsula, looking back along the craggy coastline, there are several places to park. Climb the low wall between the road and the shore and scramble down for a dip. As the road drops down from the magnificent mountain drive back towards the shore, Forge Cove, nestled in a tight sweeping curve of the road, is breathtaking in its simple beauty.

The steep drive up through the pass at Cod's Head first goes past Renisk camping B&B, intriguing with its hand-painted sign dangling out over the road that sweeps sharply around the corner. Take a photo stop and admire the fantastic views from the highest point of the pass and then continue on as the road drops back down to sea level. Soon the road circles around the gorgeous Forge Cove in a great sweeping curve. The deep crystal-clear water is hard to resist on a hot day and utterly refreshing after a long drive on these twisting and undulating roads. The tiny, whitewashed stone building at the side of the bay has 'the Forge' hand-painted on its door. A long narrow slipway runs down the centre of the pebble beach into the water.

The small slipway at the Old Forge, Beara Peninsula, County Cork

Easy access and egress at the Amphitheatre, Beara Peninsula, County Cork

Walk down the long, narrow slipway into this pristine cove. A few rowboats rest on the beach at low tide. From here, it is clear how the road just travelled seems precariously shored up with drystone walling on the opposite side of the cove.

Climb around the rocks to the left of this delightful little bay where there is a narrow cleft creating a channel that cuts through the rocks behind the pier. The cove quickly gets deep and one can enjoy a leisurely swim, cooling off after a long drive or challenging cycle ride.

For the adventure swimmer who likes jumping from rocks and challenging conditions, just a few hundred metres along this road is the 'Amphitheatre'. This deep bowl of rock and churning sea is at its best at mid to low tide. The water writhes and churns, creating whirlpools and eddies as the swell plays around the rock.

For strong swimmers only: climb along the right-hand side of the amphitheatre where a straight and narrow inlet gives the best access. Here, it is possible to jump from the rocks into deep water. The visibility is good and the rocks are stepped making it easy for an agile swimmer to climb out. The swirl of the water is immensely powerful in the 'amphitheatre' itself, even in flat-calm conditions so care should be taken not to venture too close.

The steep sides of this bowl of rock provide shelter from the wind and create a suntrap where one can spend several hours simply drinking in the sounds of the swell and the tide.

AT A GLANCE: FORGE COVE

NO FACILITIES | BOATS | ROCKS AND ROCK POOLS | EASY ACCESS

Swim in the crystal-clear waters of this roadside cove where turquoise hues light up in the autumn sunlight at this pretty little bay.

BY CAR OR BICYCLE: from Kenmare town take the R573 west along the northern shore of the Beara Peninsula. Shortly after the turn for Eyeries continue west on the R575 towards Allihies. This scenic mountain-pass drive first goes past Renisk camping B&B, with its hand-painted sign. As the road drops down and sweeps around close to the water's edge, the beach and slipway are revealed. Limited parking is on the roadside verge.

Grid ref: V 57658 46556

AT A GLANCE: AMPHITHEATRE

ADVANCED ADVENTURE SWIM, STRONG SWIMMERS ONLY | JUMPING AND DIVING WITH CARE

At mid to low tide this amphitheatre is revealed, the tide washing in and out, creating whirlpools and eddies. Climb over the rocks to the right of the amphitheatre. Here an inlet deep enough to jump from the stepped rocks provides safe access for strong swimmers and for climbing out again. Not recommended to venture into the bowl itself and great care should be taken as even on calm days the effect is somewhat like a washing machine.

BY CAR: From Forge Cove (above) drive on a few bends in the road into the townland of Dooneen on the R575 to Allihies. This curious stone theatre is visible over the low wall. A few hundred metres on, a lay-by on the left gives room to park a couple of cars. Walk back down the road, over the stone wall and climb down to the deep bowl of stone.

Grid ref: V 57754 46287

County Kerry

Derrynane, Iveragh Peninsula

Viewed from the road above, Derrynane Beach, once notorious as a smugglers' port, makes the swimmer itch to get down to it. The road is long and winding and seems to take you far past the first tantalising view but persevere and follow the signs for Derrynane House. These will eventually lead down to the shore and this gorgeous string of beaches.

Walking from the car park over the grassy bank, you will find the beaches laid out in front: a series of sandy coves, each a different size and shape. The water virtually calls out for one to run down the strand and dive right in. Picture-perfect, the white sandy beaches curve around between the scattered rocks where one can happily while away an entire day swimming and rock-pooling in this natural harbour.

As we walk along the strand, we easily find a private space, sheltered from the wind and away from other visitors, behind one of the several rock outcrops. Take care at the largest stretch of beach as it is prone to strong currents but there are plenty of coves and bays to explore and swim. Sunsets here are unparalleled, bathing the cove in pink and purple hues.

Above and facing page: The evening sun illuminates the sky at Derrynane Beach, Iveragh Peninsula, County Kerry

Derrynane House, the grounds of which lead down to the beach, is the ancestral home of Daniel O'Connell, 'The Liberator', the nineteenth-century politician who championed the cause of Catholic Emancipation. The oldest surviving part of the house was built in 1825 and the chapel was added in 1844, modelled on the ruined monastery chapel on Abbey Island. The house and gardens were opened to the public in 1967. Take in some of the history of the area and make the most of the views by walking the short distance to Abbey Island, where O'Connell's wife, Mary, is buried.

Before leaving this magical place call in at either Freddie's Bar or The Blind Piper for a pint and a sandwich to fuel the onward journey.

AT A GLANCE

FAMILY FRIENDLY | POPULAR | STRONG CURRENTS | SCENIC WALK | AMAZING SUNSETS

A beautiful natural harbour contained between Abbey Island to the west and Lamb's Head to the south, this series of separate beaches provides great bathing, best for sunsets.

At the western end of the beach a spit of sand leads on to Abbey Island and the remains of the eighth-century St Finian's Abbey.

BY CAR: only 3.5km from Caherdaniel in the south-western corner of the Iveragh Peninsula on the N70 Ring of Kerry route. At Caherdaniel look out for signs to Derrynane. Turn right at Freddie's Bar (signed for Derrynane) and pass The Blind Piper. Continue along the twisting road, past Derrynane House, where there is car parking (fees apply here – at time of writing adult admission €2.75, child €1.25 – and one can pay to tour the house) or drive to the large car park close to shore.

Grid ref: V 52582 58489

20

County Kerry

Ballinskelligs, Iveragh Peninsula

Just off the famed Ring of Kerry, the main route around the Iveragh Peninsula, is the lesser known Skelligs Ring on the south-western tip of the peninsula. Whether you are travelling by car or bike, be prepared for some steep climbs around the coastal road with mountains and lakes to one side and the impressive rugged coastline to the other. Ballinskelligs Beach is on the western side of the horseshoe-shaped bay. The beach faces into the main bay and is sheltered to the south by Horse Island.

The Iveragh Peninsula has been attracting walkers and cyclists to Kerry for many years. The famous MacGillycuddy's Reeks mountain range and the Kerry Way paths running across the peninsula are a constant draw.

Ballinskelligs (meaning 'the place of the craggy rock') is a blue flag beach but, even so, never gets really busy, as it is tucked out of the way on this western peninsula.

Looking south to the ruins of the sixteenth-century McCarthy Castle at Ballinskelligs Beach, County Kerry

The 'craggy rocks' refer to the Skellig Islands – Skellig Michael and Little Skellig – which were home to monks in the sixth century. Boat trips to the islands run from Ballinskelligs harbour.

The beach is at the western end of Ballinskelligs Bay, an almost circular bay between the promontories of Bolus Head and Hogs Head. The 1km of soft white sand shelves gradually and has clear, sheltered waters. The ruins of the sixteenth-century McCarthy castle sit on a narrow isthmus that juts out into the bay facing the beach. A great place for children young and old to explore. The remains of an old pier near the castle, several metres out from shore, is a great place from which to jump and dive at high tide. A little further along the shore are the remains of the twelfth-century Ballinskelligs Abbey.

Part of the appeal is the route to get here so take the time to explore and do some sightseeing on the way. From Valentia Island, north-west of Iveragh, continue on the Skelligs Ring, the R566. Pass the sign for 'Kerry's Most Spectacular Cliffs' as the road ahead cuts up over the mountain and down to the rugged St Finian's Bay. Right beside the road, at the Holy Well, is a small, exposed beach. At low tide the sand is revealed; at high tide jagged rocks point down to the sea. Strong currents here mean it is not good for swimming; however, there are great views out towards the craggy Skellig Rocks. Nearby is Skellig's Chocolate Factory. This family-run company welcomes visitors to its open-plan factory to watch the chocolate-making process.

AT A GLANCE

FAMILY FRIENDLY | POPULAR

A pleasant strand with castle ruins and an old abbey to explore: snorkel around the old pier searching for crabs and sea life. One can also take a boat trip to visit Skellig Michael: this ancient monastic settlement is the second of Ireland's UNESCO World Heritage sites and is a Special Protection Area for seabirds. In 2014, Star Wars descended on the island to film scenes for 'Episode 7: The Force Awakens'.

BY CAR: from the N70 Ring of Kerry at the south-west of the Iveragh peninsula, between Cahersiveen and Waterville, take the R566 towards Ballinskelligs and follow the signs to the beach and car park.

Grid ref: V 43484 65503

21

County Kerry

Glanleam, Valentia Island

Boathouses at Glanleam, Valentia Island, County Kerry

Valentia Island's own tourism website states that it is easy to find and that 'the small island known as Ireland lies to the east'. This quirkiness and sense of fun draws one to Valentia. Many visitors will take the main route and arrive in the bustling centre of Knight's Town where swimming in the harbour is popular but for a quiet and more secluded swim, take the road north-west towards Glanleam House and Gardens. From this tiny private beach you can swim between Valentia and Beginish Island or follow the coast west towards the lighthouse.

This spot is a local secret and you might meet one of the locals taking to the waters for its reputed health benefits, a tradition that has been passed down through the generations.Some swear that a regular dip keeps colds and injury at bay.

The small beach is at the bottom of a narrow lane from the road, just metres from the entrance to Glanleam House and Gardens, an old estate dating back to the 1770s which was home to five generations of the Knights of Kerry who each extended the house. The subtropical gardens are a major draw. At the beach there are two old boathouses (one of which is refurbished and available to rent out: a summer idyll, with blue flowering shrubs curling around the pathway and just a few steps from the door into the water). The small beach of grey sand melts into the water. Beginish Island lies directly in front of the bay and to the left along the shore is Valentia's lighthouse.

The swim to the lighthouse is approximately 1.25km and it is almost the same distance across to Beginish at its closest point. If you plan to swim to Beginish, have an accompanying kayak as the boats from Knight's Town use the channel between the two islands.

Nearing the north-west corner of the Iveragh peninsula, Valentia Island is a step back in time. At only 11km long by 5km wide it is perfect for cycling trips and the pretty and vibrant Knight's Town has plenty to offer by way of food and entertainment. The harbour area plays host to a half marathon event at the beginning of autumn, and, with pontoons alongside the main jetty, is also popular for swimming in the summer.

Quiet swim at Glanleam with view of Valentia Lighthouse, County Kerry

AT A GLANCE

FAMILY FRIENDLY | SECLUDED | SCENIC SWIM

Glanleam Beach – bathe at this tiny bay hidden away beneath Glanleam House and Gardens, take a longer, scenic swim along the coast to the lighthouse, rent a refurbished boathouse for a weekend to get away from it all.

BY CAR: Valentia Island is on the north-west tip of the Iveragh Peninsula. Follow the N70 Ring of Kerry to Cahersiveen, then follow the signs for the ferry.

Take the ferry from Cahersiveen to Knight's Town, a five-minute trip (at time of writing, the fee for a car was €6 one way, €9 return). Alternatively, from the N70 take the R565 to Portmagee and cross the bridge onto Valentia Island. Follow the road towards Knight's Town. At Castletown turn left and cut across the island following the signs for Glanleam House and Gardens. The beach is down a small slipway just before the house and gardens.

The ferry service from Cahersiveen runs to Knight's Town during the summer season until October.

Grid ref: V 40680 77144

Waves wash over stones at Glanleam with Beginish Island in the background, County Kerry

View of Minard Beach with the sixteenth-century Fitzgerald castle, Dingle Peninsula, County Kerry

22

County Kerry

Minard, Dingle Peninsula

The storm beach of Minard is considered one of the finest of its type in Ireland: great boulders rounded by the sea and then thrown onto the shore during storms tumble down to the waters' edge. The sand is revealed only at low tide. Prominent on the hill overlooking the bay are the remains of the sixteenth-century Minard Castle, one of three Fitzgerald castles on the peninsula.

The Dingle Peninsula on Ireland's south-west stretches 50km out into the Atlantic Ocean with the Blasket Islands on its western tip and dominated by a spine of mountains running from Slieve Mish to Mount Brandon, Ireland's second highest peak.

Writing in the sand at Minard Beach

The coastline consists of steep cliffs and many sandy beaches safe for swimming and surfing, and Minard has a special appeal. The great sandstone boulders piled on the beach have been worn smooth over the aeons and serve as a natural barrier that prevents flooding and erosion of the fields inshore. The cliffs of Minard around the bay are made of fossilised desert sand dunes, 380 million years old.

At low tide the beach is superb for swimming, with calm water and no strong currents. There are organised swimming lessons for local children during the summer months. A little bridge at the foot of the castle grounds is a popular children's paddling spot.

At high tide the sand will be all but submerged and it is the great stones which take centre stage.

The castle above the bay was once the stronghold of the Knights of Kerry. Cromwellian forces attempted to blow it up in 1650, placing charges at each corner. It withstood the blasts and three storeys of the rectangular tower still survive. However, the damage was such that it was no longer habitable, and the crumbling walls and huge breach facing the sea lie open to the ravages of weather and time.

In more recent history, Minard is where the young Tom Crean from Anascaul enlisted with the British Navy. He was a member of three major Antarctic expeditions, under Scott and Shackleton, and earned three Polar Medals. When Crean retired from the navy, he returned to Anascaul and, with his wife, opened a pub called The South Pole Inn.

Panorama of Minard Beach with its castle, looking south towards the Iveragh Peninsula

Swimming at Minard Beach

AT A GLANCE

SCENIC WALK | FAMILY FRIENDLY

Scramble over the amazing rounded boulders down to the beach at low tide, perfect for swimming in this gently shelving bay.

BY CAR: from Tralee, take the N86 to Anascaul. Minard Beach and Castle are about fifteen minutes' drive from Anascaul (or approximately a two-hour walk along quiet country roads). From Anascaul head south-west towards Dingle, then take the first left, signed for Inch. After 450 metres, turn right and follow this road to Minard Castle.

From Dingle town, take the N86 east to Lispole (approximately 8km). About 2km after Lispole turn right towards Minard. This road brings you to the beach.

Grid ref: V 55625 99246

23

County Clare

Pollock Holes, Kilkee

The diving boards near the Pollock Holes with George's Point in the background

Step out onto the Duggerna Reef at the mouth of Kilkee's horseshoe bay and walk onto a barren and exposed landscape. Steps lead down to a pile of rounded stones and, beyond the reef, revealed at low tide is a plateau of slabs of rock, smoothed by the twice-daily ebb and flow of the sea. As the sea drops away from the rocks, the magical pools are revealed, the Pollock Holes. Three good-sized pools, left full by the retreating tide and full of life.

As you slip into the still water of these sheltered pools, anemones wave their soft tentacles, stroking as you pass, in search of unseen creatures. The colourful underwater world is far removed from the hard and flat grey stone above. Even as the Atlantic rages at the edge of the reef, creating swathes of foam which blows across the pools, one can peacefully swim and snorkel, the yellows and purples of underwater plants lighting up the pale green waters.

Kilkee has been a seaside resort town for nearly 200 years, starting with the passenger steamer service in 1816 between Limerick and Kilrush. As it grew in popularity the West Clare Railway was built in the late 1800s and the area has been popular ever since.

Inside the bay the crescent-shaped beach, sheltered by the Duggerna Reef, has drawn holidaymakers since those early days; look out for the monochrome portrait of Che Guevara on the beach wall.

Many celebrities have visited over the years since the Victorians: Charlotte Brontë Alfred, Lord Tennyson and William Makepeace Thackeray. Actor Richard Harris had a holiday home here and played in the local racquets club (he was champion from 1948–51 and there is a statue to him above the reef).

The poet and composer Percy French often entertained here in packed-out venues. His song 'Are ye right there, Michael?' was written about the West Clare Railway after a delayed rail journey caused French to miss a concert. The popular ballad was of great embarrassment and the rail company took libel action. It is said the case was thrown out when French arrived late for the hearing, his apology being: 'Your Honour, I travelled by the West Clare Railway.'

Left and following spread: The Pollock Holes offer shelter from a wild Atlantic Ocean

To reach the Duggerna Reef and Pollock Holes, follow the road out of town around the left side of the bay, passing a small white-painted changing area with a long staircase down to the water. The road swings away from the beach, then curves to the left where there is a small gap in the wall beside another squat and square white building. Here you might take the side trip to visit the diving platforms. The steps narrow as they round the little building, leading down to two concrete diving plinths. The boards are long removed and signs are up to say that diving is not safe. However, it is clear that this spot has been used by divers for generations. The water is deep here at the cliffs and a single ladder is provided for your exit climb.

For the reef, continue to the end of the road and the large car park at the Diamond Rocks Café. The Pollock Holes are directly in front, revealed at low tide. If you have arrived early and need to kill some time, take a walk around the headland for spectacular views and watch the waves explode as they hit the reef. Traditionally the nearest pool was for ladies only and the farthest was for men, but now they are mixed and increasingly popular for snorkelling.

These pools have become an institution and although well known (and therefore busy) during summer, they are well worth the visit. Warm up in the café with scones and hot coffee after your swim.

AT A GLANCE

FAMILY FRIENDLY | ROCK POOLS | JUMPING WITH CARE | LOW TIDE ONLY | SNORKELLING

Swim midst the amazing sea life caught in these rock pools revealed at low tide. Follow it with the exhilarating rush of jumping from high boards along the cliffs and finish the day with a stroll along the crescent-shaped sheltered beach, all within this one bay.

BY CAR: from Ennis, take the N68 to Kilrush, then the N67 to Kilkee. The Pollock Holes are located just outside Kilkee. To reach them, drive through the town and at the roundabout take the L2009, signposted Coast Road. Follow this road as it winds along the western side of the bay until you reach the car park. The rocks can be slippery as you walk out. Beware of the incoming tide as the outer rocks get cut off quite quickly.

Grid ref: Q 88114 60139

County Galway

Blackrock Diving Tower, Salthill

Blackrock Diving Tower, Salthill, County Galway

From the vibrant musical bustle of Galway city's street pubs and performers it is a short step to the hills of Connemara and the beaches of the west of Ireland. From the city centre one can walk 2km along the promenade to Blackrock and Salthill's famous diving boards, where you will meet a population of hardy swimmers and divers who regularly fling themselves from the high board, whatever the weather.

Salthill Diving Boards, Blackrock Tower bathing area, Salthill, County Galway

The bathing area and boards are like a magnet, drawing young and old, and are a hive of activity as retirees mix with schoolchildren to swim and jump from the dual-aspect platforms. The boards have become a rite of passage for school leavers. On the final day of term before the summer holidays they flock en masse to the Blackrock Diving Tower area and climb the steps to charge off the highest board.

A thirty-minute walk from the centre of town brings you to this iconic Galway swimming hole: Salthill's diving boards on Blackrock Tower. The walls are built at strategic angles to provide shelter from the wind for dressing and a long, low bench serves as seating. A wide crescent of steps leads down into the sea at the bathing section, behind the diving boards. A narrow staircase rises up the centre of the structure to the top diving platform where divers gather their nerve before taking the plunge.

Join the local swimmers who will happily guide you to the very best places to visit and shower you with stories of the area.

As you walk the promenade between Salthill and Galway city look out for quotes from the Nobel Prize-winning poet Seamus Heaney embedded in the walls and on the pavement or visit the National Aquarium of Ireland, Galway Atlantaquaria, on the prom. End your day back in the vibrant city with its wide variety of restaurants and pubs with live music.

AT A GLANCE

FAMILY FRIENDLY | JUMPING WITH CARE | POPULAR

Join the locals in this popular bathing area and dive from the dual-aspect boards which have featured in several films, including Brendan Gleeson's 'The Guard'.

BY CAR: take the road from Galway city towards Salthill. There is car parking at various points along the 2km promenade. The bathing area is found at the far end.

BY FOOT: from Galway city, walk along the promenade, approximately thirty minutes from the city.

Grid ref: M 27199 23526

Above and facing page: Early morning dip with the dog at Trá Sailín, County Galway

25

Trá Sailín, Spiddal

From Galway city the coast road through Salthill and Barna runs alongside a string of beaches, some popular and some hardly known. The main beaches each have good car parking but can be busy during the summer season. Take the time to explore one of the many single-track lanes off the shore road to find your own private beach. One such cove is Trá Sailín: Salty Beach, the perfect spot to pitch your tent on the grass and take a quiet moonlight dip.

Swim from the tiny beach, turning left around the rocky outcrop into the brackish mix where a stream flowing in meets the salt water of the bay. As you swim, look due south across the bay to the Burren in County Clare and west to the Aran Islands, hazy in the morning light.

The small beach affords a pleasant dip, shallow as you walk out and hemmed in on each side by the rocks reaching out into Galway Bay. After your swim take a walk along the shore to warm up.

It is said that the month of September is a particularly good month to swim in the sea as it is then that the seaweeds release their nutrients, which are reputedly very good for the skin. Sailín is well known as a good spot for the collection of seaweed at that time of the year.

Sailín cove is a place of quiet solitude where calmness pervades the air. To the left, between the stream and the beach, is a small bracken-covered hillock, fenced around. This is protected ground, a graveyard for children who died in the Great Famine between 1845 and 1852. Locals still pay respect to their memory.

AT A GLANCE

SKINNY-DIPPING | SECLUDED | WILD CAMPING | BEACH FISHING

Wild camping at this tiny, private cove. Swim in the brackish river around to the beach looking out across Galway Bay towards County Clare and the Aran Islands.

BY CAR OR BICYCLE: take the R336 west from Galway city, through Barna and Spiddal. Look out for the small brown signpost for Trá Sailín pointing to the single-track lane that leads to a small turning circle with parking room for four cars. Pitch on the grass above high water and take a late evening or early morning dip. .

Grid ref: M 10266 21973

26

County Galway

Trá an Doilín/the Coral Beach

At the mouth of Galway Bay, wedged between Casla Bay and Greatman's Bay lies one of the most extraordinary beaches in Ireland: Carraroe's Coral Beach, or Trá an Dóilín. This unusual beach is made not of sand but of what looks like tiny pieces of coral in myriad colours. Scoop a handful and it gleams with the mother-of-pearl of tiny snail shells, minute cornet shells and minuscule pieces of coral, the colours ranging from purple, orange, yellow and fading to pure sun-bleached white.

The area at the mouth of Galway Bay is a series of islands, some joined by causeways to the mainland. There are several almost deserted beaches to be found by following the winding roads down to old disused turf quays, Trá an Dóilín has a special appeal and is one not to miss. This series of small coves nestled between rocky outcrops are filled with coralline algae known as maerl. The tiny branches of delicate underwater plants mingle with hair-fine algae, rich in purple and red hues all heaped together in their millions, along with the most minute seashells you could hope to find, creating this fascinating beach.

Tread carefully as you explore the rock pools and coves because maerl, while beautiful, is sharp on bare feet. It crunches beneath you as you walk. As you swim in the clear water those countless colours beneath catch the light.

Above: Trá an Dóilín, looking out to Gentleman's Bay, County Galway

Facing page inset: Scoop a handful and it gleams with the mother-of-pearl of tiny snail shells, minute cornet shells and minuscule pieces of coral, at Trá an Dóilín

Each little cove is sheltered and perfect for swimming, the rocks on either side reaching out and protecting the tiny bays from any strong currents. You can happily make your way along the coast by swimming from one cove to the next. The water is clear and shelves fairly quickly.

Here, too, you may be lucky enough to see a Galway Hooker, the native Irish boat topped with its distinctive dark red sail. These boats were traditionally used for both fishing and hauling turf from Connemara to the Aran Islands, but now are mostly used for racing.

Spend an afternoon here rock-pooling and beachcombing, just remember your beach shoes!

Although the first bay you come to is overlooked by the car park, there are plenty more small coves and beaches between the rocky outcrops where one can find a secluded spot to swim.

AT A GLANCE

SNORKELLING | ROCK POOLS | POPULAR | TOILET FACILITIES

Carraroe's Coral Beach is made entirely of coralline algae, of vibrant colours ranging from bleached white to deep purple. Watch the famous Galway Hookers sail across the bay. The August bank holiday sees Féile an Dóilín, a Galway Hooker festival. Trá an Dóilín has plenty of rock-pooling and nooks and crannies to get away from the crowds. Several small coves between rocky outcrops provide quiet swimming. Sandals recommended as the tiny pieces of maerl can be sharp on sensitive feet.

BY CAR: from Galway city take the R336 coast road west past Connemara airport. At Casla, turn left onto the R343 and follow the signs for Carraroe. Drive through the village and look for the signpost for Trá an Dóilín, which brings you to the car park and beach.

Grid ref: L 91301 22996

27

Dog's Bay and Gurteen, Roundstone

Jumping into the sand at an unnamed beach on Dog's Bay, County Galway

In the pretty village of Roundstone, art galleries and studios for handmade ceramics and jewellery vie for space, and a walk through the town will bring you to craft shops and a good variety of bars, restaurants and cafés, which serve locally caught seafood. The multicoloured terraced houses crowd the road opposite the deep harbour, while fuchsia plants bob their red heads over the wall in the breeze. On the road out towards Gurteen and Dog's Bay, surly sheep lie warming themselves on the tarmac, oblivious to the occasional car trying to negotiate a way around them.

The road signs from Roundstone will bring you past Dog's Bay Caravan Park and then down a lane to a parking area at the first of four beaches on the west of this hammerhead-shaped tombolo, Dog's Bay, where the smooth horseshoe beach is backed by a grass bank where cattle wander freely.

Taking a clockwise tour from this first beach, Dog's Bay, cross the narrow spit of land that forms the neck of the tombolo to Gurteen's long and sweeping bay. Gurteen is almost a kilometre long with the caravan park at the north-east end of the beach. Both of these beaches are ideal for swimming: if the wind is too strong at Dog's Bay it is likely that Gurteen will be sheltered. However, this is not all the area has to offer.

View across Dog's Bay towards Funachree

Gurteen with Inis Leacan in the background

Continue clockwise from the southern end of Gurteen and walk west approximately 300 metres over the delicate grasslands, made up of rare machair vegetation, a habitat found on the west coasts of Ireland and Scotland, to the quiet third beach. The same fine white sand can be found on this raw and exposed beach, where the wind has eaten away the edge of the dunes and the ancient fencing has fallen. Few people walk this far past the docile cattle yet the reward is a pretty strand all to oneself. Set between two banks of rock and facing almost due south this small strand is a super swim; to the right of the bay the rocks hide a deep narrow inlet.

From here continue your loop walk north-northwest another 400 metres to the fourth and final treat of the day, a narrow, almost hidden, gully with a steep bank of soft sand gouged into the high grass banks.

As you swim out around the rocks to the east of this little cove you can see the horseshoe strand of Dog's Bay, where we began. It is a mere 240-metre walk east over the rise from this narrow cove back to Dog's Bay beach.

An arrow points the way to unnamed third beach, facing south on the tombolo, at Gurteen and Dog's Bay

AT A GLANCE

SCENIC WALK | FAMILY FRIENDLY | SECLUDED

From an inauspicious start point, the beaches of Dog's Bay and Gurteen are glorious with fine, pure white sand, lying back to back with just a narrow spit of grassland between them. Discover two more hidden beaches across the bulbous nose of this tombolo. A sign maps the beaches on the tombolo of which there are four.

BY CAR: take the N59 north-west from Galway city, then turn left onto the R341 to Roundstone. Follow the signs to Dog's Bay Caravan Park. Continue past the caravan park to a rough track leading to a parking area (at the time of writing, work was ongoing here, with new gravel being laid beside the old and rusty fencing).

BY BUS: Bus Éireann's Clifden-to-Galway route serves Roundstone daily during summer and three days a week in the winter.

Grid refs:

Dog's Bay: L 69375 38626

Gurteen: L 69683 38229

Third beach: L 69112 37723

Fourth narrow cove: L 68914 38131

The horseshoe strand of Gurteen, County Galway

Small jellies near Glassilaun Beach, County Galway

28

County Galway

Glassilaun, Connemara

Connemara has its own raw beauty – lake-dotted peat bogs and myriad beaches made from stone, shell and fine white sand – and as one travels towards Killary Fjord the mountains soar up in rugged green banks from the roadside, making one want to jump out of the car and stride into the hills, despite driving rain. The narrow, winding roads weave through the landscape past tiny fisherman's huts, some looking like miniature whitewashed stone cottages. Near the mouth of the deep glacial fjord of Killary Harbour is the pretty Glassilaun Beach.

Glassilaun Beach, facing Inishdegil More, County Galway

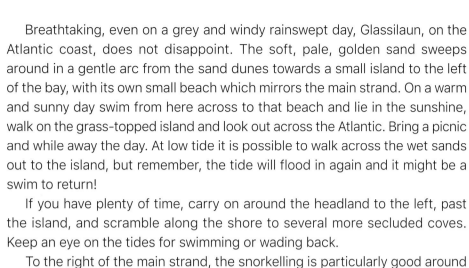

Breathtaking, even on a grey and windy rainswept day, Glassilaun, on the Atlantic coast, does not disappoint. The soft, pale, golden sand sweeps around in a gentle arc from the sand dunes towards a small island to the left of the bay, with its own small beach which mirrors the main strand. On a warm and sunny day swim from here across to that beach and lie in the sunshine, walk on the grass-topped island and look out across the Atlantic. Bring a picnic and while away the day. At low tide it is possible to walk across the wet sands out to the island, but remember, the tide will flood in again and it might be a swim to return!

If you have plenty of time, carry on around the headland to the left, past the island, and scramble along the shore to several more secluded coves. Keep an eye on the tides for swimming or wading back.

To the right of the main strand, the snorkelling is particularly good around the rocks in the deep channel. Towards Killary Bay Little and Saltrock, just north of this channel, beyond a narrow spit of land is Killary Harbour glacial fjard (similar to a fjord, but shorter, shallower and broader). At 16km long and over 45 metres deep it is one of three fjards in Ireland (Belfast and Carlingford Loughs being the others). Killary is known for its seafood so, on your return trip, call at one of the roadside stands for fresh mussels.

AT A GLANCE

FAMILY FRIENDLY | SCENIC WALK | SNORKELLING

From Glassilaun beach, swim across the beautiful bay to a tiny island with its mini beach, snorkel east, west and north into Killary Bay Little or at low tide explore the hidden coves around the headland.

BY CAR: from Clifden take the N59 toward Westport. Pass through Kylemore, then turn left, signposted for Tullycross. Drive along this road, passing two lakes: Lough Fee and Lough Muck. After the second lake, watch for a sharp right turn, signposted Scuba World, which will bring you to the car park and short walk through the dunes to the beach.

Grid ref: L 75913 64486

29

County Mayo

Keem, Achill Island

A visit to Achill Island on the west coast of County Mayo takes one a step back in time to idyllic childhood summers where all day was spent on the beach and treats were an ice cream 'poke' and a fish-and-chip supper. One of the most beautiful beaches on Achill is the picturesque Keem Beach at the western end of the island. The first view of the beach is from the vertiginous road that winds up from Dooagh village. This horseshoe bay, set in a steep amphitheatre under Benmore cliffs, is said to have been blessed by St Patrick. With the sun lighting up the deep water, the colours range from a bright turquoise darkening to teal green against the vibrant bright green grass on the slopes of Benmore.

Although a popular beach, Keem is never crowded, even at the height of the tourist season.

Go down the steep, winding road to the beach and find a quiet spot. Swim around the rocks to the left of the beach where at low tide there are several secluded sandy coves revealed. Up on the cliff someone has painted 'nudist' on the rocks, however, it is unclear, whether this is a designated 'au naturel' swimming area or not.

Walkers will enjoy the climb up Croaghaun behind the beach, which affords more spectacular

Keem Beach, County Mayo

Moyteoge Head with Keem Beach, Achill Island

views, before heading west to the cliffs of Benmore (possibly the highest sea cliffs in Ireland: the debate rages on). No matter, they are superb on a clear day.

Looking down to the beach, think of the challenges the local fishermen used to face. It was from this strand that they would set out in their curraghs, the traditional canvas-covered boats used up until the 1940s and 1950s, in search of basking sharks. The oil of the basking shark was an important source of income for the islanders. Now tourism is Achill's chief business.

Crossing onto the island separated from the mainland by a single bridge, the road onto Achill goes through the peat bog landscape towards the village of Keel. The roads taper and black-faced sheep wander unconcerned along the tarmac. These narrow roads and unhurried atmosphere makes the island well suited to cycling trips. The campsite at Keel is well equipped, although can be busy in the summer. Surfing is popular here and the long strand is a moment's walk from the campsite.

Take a bicycle or car and travel around the island, visit the Deserted Village and walk in the hills.

Keem Beach, Achill Island

AT A GLANCE

POPULAR | FAMILY FRIENDLY | SNORKELLING

Keem beach – swim where fishermen launched their curraghs in search of basking sharks. Follow the main Achill road, R319, through Dooagh village and climb above the coast for spectacular views down to Keem. Quieter to the left-hand side of the beach. Walk up the ridge onto Croaghaun Mountain and enjoy the spectacular views from the Benmore Cliffs.

BY CAR: take the R319 across Achill, through the villages of Keel and Dooagh. The road leads directly to Keem beach, ending at a car park above the beach.

Grid ref: F 56126 04323

30

County Mayo

Lough Nakeeroge and Annagh Bay

The first view of Lough Nakeeroge is unexpected: a pretty lake in the shadow of Croaghaun Mountain, protected by steep cliffs. The lowest corrie lake in Ireland, it is just 16 metres above sea level and is separated from the sea by a narrow bridge of grass and heather. Close by are the remains of a booley village (a village occupied for part of the year usually to allow livestock to graze on fresh pastures), including a beehive-shaped stone building at the western end of the strand.

There are many tales of ghostly apparitions at Annagh so those of a super-stitious nature should avoid camping here.

Following the cycle loop from Keel, turn right at the Minaun Bar for the road inland to the Deserted Village. This site dates back through several stages in history: there is a Neolithic tomb, indicating that the area was inhabited some 5,000 years ago. The remains we now see are of the village abandoned during the famine in 1845, more than 100 stone cottages in the shelter of Slievemore Mountain left to fall to ruin.

To find the gorgeous Lough Nakeeroge and Annagh Bay, park your car or bicycle at the graveyard and follow the track past the village up on towards the quarry. Quartz stone litters the path and on a sunny day patches of rock blaze white against the green and purple heather.

From the quarry continue uphill on the rough track towards Slievemore Signal tower, a small square building on top of the hill, from which there are wonderful views across the island looking back towards Keel. Continue climbing over the next rise, keeping Slievemore to your back. At the top you are rewarded with your first view of Lough Nakeeroge and Annagh Bay. There are no roads here: the only way in or out is to walk or travel by boat to Annagh Bay and you will probably have it all to yourself. After a

Looking west over Lough Nakeeroge and Annagh Bay with Saddle Head in the distance, County Mayo

long walk on a hot day, the lough is a beautiful freshwater swim, right next to the sea. Remember to give yourself time before darkness falls for the steep climb back up and your return to the Deserted Village, a good hour's walk. Keep an eye on the weather conditions, too, because the mist can drop down quickly from Slievemore. If you have less time, the eastern end of Annagh Bay is a shorter walk: from the quarry veer right and continue over the low ridge between Slievemore and the signal tower. As the shore comes into view there is a craggy cove to the right. Several inlets cut into the rocks here are great for jumping. Scramble over the rocks into deep water and explore the coastline where cormorants fish and seagulls wheel overhead. This is an adventure swim for the strong swimmer and care should be taken to swim only in calm conditions.

AT A GLANCE: ANNAGH BAY

SCENIC WALK | SNORKELLING | SECLUDED & REMOTE | JUMPING WITH CARE | ROCKS AND HAZARDS | DIFFICULT PATH | ADVENTURE SWIM

Walk through heather and quartz in this bog land to a rocky cove for an adventure swim with jumping. Care should be taken to swim only in calm conditions. Strong swimmers only.

BY CAR : from Keel on the R319, turn at the Minaun Bar onto the Slievemore Road and follow the signs to the Deserted Village. Park here and follow the track past the village to the quarry, veer right and continue over the ridge with Slievemore on the right and the signal tower on the left. It is a forty-minute walk from the Deserted Village; no road access.

Grid ref: F 62362 07787

AT A GLANCE: LOUGH NAKEEROGE

ADVENTURE SWIM | SCENIC WALK | BEACH CAMPING | DIFFICULT PATH | SECLUDED & REMOTE

A mountain walk to swim in a freshwater lough mere metres from the Atlantic waters.

BY CAR: as above to the Deserted Village. Park here. It is an hour's walk to the lough. Follow the rough track up through the quarry towards the signal tower on the hill above. Continue over the next mountain from which the first view of Lough Nakeeroge appears. No road access.

Grid ref: F 59995 07476

31

County Mayo

Pollacappul, Belmullet

Pollacappul Beach with Benwee Head in the background, County Mayo

This hidden gem is tucked away down a long laneway, and absolutely stunning. As you crest the hill on this rough single-track lane through farmland, look to the right to see the breathtaking vista of this secluded beach. Cross an old concrete stile and a field to a second stile, which leads onto the beach.

Swimming at one of Pollacappul's small coves, County Mayo

The water is clear, shallow and gently shelving; a small cave to the left provides shelter on windy days and, if you swim out around these rocks to the left of the beach, there is a tiny narrow cove: perfect for naked sunbathing. Sitting here, you will see an arch in front. At low tide it is possible to walk through. Is this tiny cove a jellyfish nursery? Iridescence flashes from the jelly-babies as they catch the sunlight, turning in the gentle tides. Few people venture to this less-popular part of the Mullet Peninsula and this beach, tucked as it is so far off the beaten track, will probably be completely deserted, leaving you to enjoy the tranquil solitude of this gorgeous bay.

Rather than taking the main road south on the Mullet Peninsula, turn instead north-east and take the less-travelled route, away from the majority of tourists, towards Baile Glas Lighthouse. This road winds between rolling hills and just before Baile Glas, look to the left for the small brown sign for Pollacappul. The single-track road goes along the shore to a farm from where there is a stony lane up over the hill. At the top of the hill the beach is revealed, tantalisingly close just below the fields to the right. Here the track is wide enough to pull a car into the side and allow any other vehicle to pass (rare though that will be). Park beside the concrete stile and follow the fence down to the beach.

Bring a picnic for this trip as once you get here, if the weather is good, you will not want to leave. Having this pristine beach all to oneself to swim and sunbathe and laze the day away – bliss!

AT A GLANCE

SECLUDED | SKINNY-DIPPING | SCENIC WALK

A perfect secluded beach to skinny-dip and sunbathe, miles from the tourist crowds. There are rocks to climb along the coast and inlets to explore.

BY CAR OR BICYCLE: cross the bridge from Belmullet and follow the R313 travelling north towards Baile Glas. The road bends sharply right and continues for several kilometres. At the sign for Pollacappul Rock and Beach Fishing, turn left down a single-track road. Continue past the farmhouse where the tarmac runs out; the rough lane goes further up through the farmland. Pull in close to the fence at the stone stile and walk the track down to the beach.

Grid ref: F 75088 36615

View from Pollacappul headland towards Ballyglass, County Mayo

32

County Mayo

Portacloy

One of the most scenic places along the north-west Mayo coast is pretty Portacloy. This beautiful bay, off the main R314 route from Belderg to Belmullet, is hidden between Port Durlainne and Carrowteige. The sheltered white-sand beach lies in a natural harbour created by two headlands stretching out on either side. Safe from the Atlantic swell, this pretty little beach is the perfect place to camp, enjoy swims across the bay or take the scenic walk over the headland to Carrowteige.

Portacloy's Green Coast beach sits virtually empty with white cottages dotting the hillside and sheep grazing on the surrounding fields. On the approach to Portacloy a large stone on the roadside is handsomely engraved, welcoming visitors to the cove.

Portacloy Beach: the view north towards Benwee Head, County Mayo

And that is all there is: no shop, no streets, just a winding road that runs down to a short, sandy lane onto the beach. The road carries on to the left to the small pier. Park on the sandy lane beside a small football field which houses a portacabin, where wetsuits hanging out to dry are the only clue that the beach is used at all. As you walk onto the stunning beach, completely sheltered in this natural harbour, you wonder why no one else is here. The water is clear, the sand soft and white, shelving gradually, which makes it ideal for all levels of swimmer.

To the left, on the western side of the bay, there is an old slipway and pier where one can jump into deeper water; beyond, over the rocks, a narrow cut has created an inlet, in the centre of which a stream runs off the moorland above, the peaty water cascading into the sea. From the pier, trail markers guide you on a loop walk along the cliffs which link to Carrowteige on the far side of the headland. The full loop walk of Benwee Head, taking in the Children of Lir sculpture, is 10km, and passes lines of turf laid out to dry in the sun.

The perfect place to while away a few days, swimming and exploring the cove, scrambling over the rocks and plunging into the narrow inlet.

Portacloy Beach: the view northeast towards Knockadaff, County Mayo

Carrowteige Beach and sand dunes are another great place to camp: it is possible to drive up to the low dune system, where little grass-topped, sandy hummocks create a maze of pitching spots, sheltered from the wind and prying eyes. Take the time to do one of the three loop walks from Carrowteige. The trailhead is at Carrowteige Summer School beside Garvin's grocery and hardware store. These cliff-edge trails give great views over Broadhaven Bay's rocky islands, the Children of Lir Loop at 10km, the Black Ditch Loop at 13km or green arrows direct you on a shorter loop.

AT A GLANCE

SCENIC WALK | FAMILY FRIENDLY | BEACH CAMPING | JUMPING WITH CARE

A gem of a place with everything – beach, rocky crags, wild camping, jumping and headland walk. From the pier at Portacloy the Carrowteige Loop Walk goes over the headland and, on the approach, a mere 100 metres from the second pier, is the inlet.

BY CAR: from Ballina head north-west along the R314, through Killala, Ballycastle and Belderg. The road then drops away from the coast before coming to a right turn towards Ceathrú Thaidhg (Carrowteige). Follow the signs for Ceathrú Thaidhg Loop, turn right onto a narrow road and soon pass a rock on roadside inscribed 'Portacloy'. Go straight down this road and around a sharp left-hand bend. A short sandy track leads to the beach. There is limited parking in the laneway.

Grid ref: F 84064 43969

33

County Sligo

Aughris Head

Twenty minutes west of Sligo, turn off the main road and travel down the narrow and twisting rural lanes to the lovely Aughris Head Beach Bar. This pretty, single-storey thatched building serves superb food. An eclectic mix of décor inside and friendly staff make this a popular place with locals and returning holidaymakers. There is a long and stony beach here but the better beach by far is a 25-minute walk from here on the Aughris Head walk.

It is an ideal place for birdwatchers as small birds flit across the grassy path as you stroll along. Brambles line the fence and autumn is a good time for blackberry gathering. The path follows the rocky coastline and looking back towards the Beach Bar affords superb views across Sligo Bay to Benbulben Mountain. After about twenty minutes, the path broadens and a length of wooden fence leads down to the first of two rocky inlets calling out to be explored. The second has a stony beach providing easy access to the water.

Swimming around the north-west rocks to a second cove which is accessible only by swimming from the beach or by boat, Aughris Head, County Sligo

Facing page and this page: Aughris Head, County Sligo

Five minutes further along the path it again broadens out before sweeping around to the left above a curved black-sand beach. Tiny starfish lie washed up on the shore, bright white against the dark sand. From this beach one can swim around the rocky headland on the left into a second cove. Accessible only either by swimming or by boat, this cove feels far removed from the rest of the world. As you swim around, feel the surge of the water rushing back and forth between the shore and the rocks. Take care making your way through the narrow gap.

In this second cove, low tide reveals shallow caves under the overhanging rocks to explore. Dive under the low arches to swim under the rock walls from one cave into another – if you are brave enough!

To get to the start of the walk, follow the road up from the bar to the crossroads, turn right and walk to the small harbour, where the road sweeps sharply to the left with a sign warning cars of the steep slipway. A bungalow is directly ahead. Between the slipway and the bungalow is the start of the walk, the grass path is well mown and a fence keeps walkers safe from the edge.

The path continues to a holy well, crossing cattle fields. Return by the same path back to the Beach Bar, where you can while away the night in the popular pub and even pitch your tent in the garden for a small fee.

AT A GLANCE

SCENIC WALK | FAMILY FRIENDLY | BEACH CAMPING | JUMPING WITH CARE

A coastal walk then a swim from one cove to the next, finally return to the Beach Bar for a great meal and a pint then settle down for the night camping in the bar's beach-front garden.

Small campsite with basic facilities, it can be a little noisy depending on who's in the pub, but a very friendly atmosphere.

BY CAR: take the N4 south from Sligo town. Exit onto the N59 at Ballysadare towards Ballina, approximately 13km along this road. Aughris Head and the Beach Bar are signposted.

Grid refs:
Start of Aughris Head walk: G 50822 36232
Black-sand beach: G 50840 36801

34

County Sligo

Rosses Point and Drumcliff

Sligo town is steeped in history and mythology, a creative, vibrant place of art, music and poetry. Its lakes, beaches, mountains and ancient sites have inspired generations of stories and adventure. Visit the city for a pleasant day of meandering through narrow streets of music and wonderful wool shops and perhaps visit the wood sculptor on Main Street who will regale you with stories whilst carving the most exquisite animal sculptures.

North-west from Sligo town is the popular Rosses Point, a bustling holiday town with a thriving yacht club. Beside the yacht club, a juxtaposition of walls and steps forms an open sea pool where families of all ages enjoy the summer weather, children run along the low walls while others swim or dive in the pool.

Close by, the Metal Man stands 3.6 metres tall on a pillar on top of Perch Rock with the strong current sweeping below his feet, he points to the safe deep channel

between Rosses Point and Coney Island to guide approaching boats. He has stood here since 1821. It is said that occasionally he walks back to shore for a drink, but he must have been in a hurry to return to his post – check out his mis-buttoned tunic.

If you prefer a longer swim then enter the water here and strike out to the right, across the 1.5km bay, which spans the two sandy beaches. To the left and around the point towards the yacht club, the currents are very strong and not safe for swimming.

The pool and the first beach can be busy on summer days, but walk a little further along the shore to the second beach where there will be far fewer people. For a very secluded swim, walk across the full length of this second beach alongside the golf course and over the north headland to a third, almost deserted beach, which sits on the spit of land that juts north from Rosses Point across Drumcliff Bay. Several tracks weave through the dunes and lead down to the estuary where in the shallow waters you may witness a strange, magical scene: daisies growing underwater beside seaweed, hermit crabs carrying their tiny shells through the grass and the sun shining through the shallow, briny water, creating a haze of gold underfoot.

On your return to the main road, take the N15 to Drumcliff and visit the grave of W. B. Yeats under the shadow of Benbulben.

Drumcliff Bay with Benbulbin in the background, County Sligo

Top left and above: Rosses Point
Left and top: Drumcliff

AT A GLANCE

POPULAR | SEA POOLS AND BEACHES | STRONG CURRENTS | SCENIC WALK

See the Metal Man at Rosses Point; dip and jump in the open-sea pool or stretch out on a long swim across the bay's two sandy beaches. Or walk across the dunes to the mouth of the estuary.

BY CAR: Take the R291 north-west from Sligo town to Rosses Point, where there is plenty of car parking space. Walk past the yacht club to the point and the sea pool. Strong currents lie to the left, on the yacht club side, but to the right, towards the beaches the bay is safe to swim.

Grid refs:
Rosses Point: G 62509 39922
Drumcliff Bay: G 63255 41942

35

Bishop's Pool and Mermaid's Cove

Take a walk, run or cycle along the rugged cliffs of Mullaghmore Head, where the Wild Atlantic Way lives up to its name. The Loop Road goes past a local favourite: Bishop's Pool. At high tide the Atlantic floods in to create this tidal pool, large enough for swimming and deep enough for jumping and diving. This rock pool brims full of sea life, a perfect nursery with mini starfish and tiny crabs creeping amongst the anemones and baby eels, less than an inch long, scooting through the water and leaping out of the way when disturbed.

Bishop's Pool, County Sligo

This is probably the worst-kept 'secret swimming' place because locals and visitors alike flock here at high tide and the place is a hive of activity. The rock pool bustles with generations of swimmers and divers. The stepped rocks provide hours of scrambling with various heights to jump from into the deep pool. Great swathes of green carpet weed cascade over the black rocks and highlight the ruggedness of the place.

At low tide there is still the opportunity to do some rock-pooling, hunting for shrimp and minute sea creatures in the shallow pools left behind.

The isolated Cassiebawn Castle stands out on the skyline, perched alone on the exposed and barren Mullaghmore Head behind. Mermaids' Cove can be seen across the bay on the other side of Mullaghmore town. Its quiet family-friendly beach, only twenty minutes from the busy surfing mecca of Bundoran, is a great place to swim, snorkel and bodyboard. It suits its whimsical name as the beach is dotted with rocks and caves which may well hide some of the elusive mythical creatures in the dimming twilight.

Spend an evening out on Mullaghmore Head watching the light change and listening to the crash of the ocean. Feel the ground shake with the immense power of the Atlantic swell as the huge Atlantic rollers, known as prowlers, crash onto Mullaghmore Head. Unsurprisingly, this is one of the best big-wave surfing locations in the world.

AT A GLANCE

FAMILY FRIENDLY | POPULAR | BEACH SWIM | JUMPING WITH CARE

Jumping and diving in the Bishop's Pool, rock pool at low tide, then head across the bay to swim and surf at Mermaids' Cove.

BY CAR: north of Sligo town and close to Bundoran on the N15 take the R279 at Cliffoney towards Mullaghmore. Follow the road to the entrance to Mermaids' Cove and park on the roadside.

For Bishop's Pool take the Loop Road through Mullaghmore, keeping to the right around the headland. Stop at the small gravel parking bay with a well-tended grass picnic area and walk down the grassy bank to the large rock pool.

BY BUS: the nearest bus stop is at Cliffoney, approximately 5km from Mullaghmore. Bus Éireann operates local and Expressway services.

Grid ref: G 70803 58203

36

County Donegal

Silver Strand, Malin Beg

Silver Strand, Malin Beg, County Donegal

On the far western shores of Donegal, not far from the great cliffs of Slieve League, sits the pretty curve of Silver Strand at Malin Beg, 400 metres of golden sand beside a small harbour favoured by divers.

Silver Strand

Malin Beg Harbour is a prime underwater diving site

Venture west from Donegal town, along the N59, through the towns of Inver and Killybegs, which both have popular beaches, towards the impressive Slieve League, which is among the highest of the sea cliffs in Ireland and, at over 600 metres, rivals the Cliffs of Moher. To the south the rock has been carved by the sea and weather to form a knife-like edge rising to the summit. The road winds up to a viewpoint close to the top overlooking majestic Donegal Bay. Far below, the Giant's Desk and Giant's Chair are two rock formations easily identifiable in the cove.

The ridge walk One Man's Path requires a good head for heights as the path narrows, traversing each peak towards the summit, while the easier Pilgrim's Path winds up from the car park. Swimming, however, is not to be found here so make a full day of it with a visit to Glencolmcille and then on to finish the day at the beautiful Silver Strand.

At Glencolmcille the Folk Village is a living history museum with thatched cottages, a schoolhouse and tiny pub-grocer. It is a replica of an Irish rural village, designed and built by the local people and overlooking the beach at Glen Bay. The cottages show how people would have lived in the eighteenth, nineteenth and early twentieth centuries.

Six kilometres from Glencolmcille is Silver Strand. It is a steep climb down the steps from the car park to the enticing white sands of the horseshoe-shaped bay but worth every bit of effort. Approximately 400 metres long and with gently shelving waters, this beach provides excellent swimming and set as it is down such a flight of steps, the strand is never crowded. Nestled beneath the grassy headlands it is as close to a perfect beach as you are likely to find.

The nearby harbour at Malin Beg is rich in sea life, making it popular with divers and snorkellers. The harbour is set in a neat natural cove so it is extremely well sheltered. Swim from the harbour steps, turning right towards the small sea stack, a distance of about 90 metres, and look out along the shore on the right: just beyond the cottage there is an archway leading to a tiny gravel beach. It is always exciting to explore the darkness of a cave or arch. The tiny beach itself is sunken down behind the road and looks a little like a grotto.

AT A GLANCE

SCENIC WALK | STEEP STEPS TO BEACH | HARBOUR AND COVE TO SWIM OR SNORKEL | SEA ARCH TO TINY SHALE BEACH | HOSTEL AND CAFÉ NEARBY | FAMILY FRIENDLY

The magnificent curved beach of Silver Strand close to the sheer cliffs of Slieve League. Be prepared for the steep climb back up the steps to the car park. Snorkel at Malin Beg Harbour where there is abundant sea life, or duck through the arch to the right of the harbour to a minute gravel beach.

BY CAR: from Donegal town take the N56 west along the shore of Donegal Bay, then the R263 through Killybegs. Carry on along the R263 to Glencolmcille with its two beaches, the smaller of which is more private.

For Silver Strand, continue on the R263 from Glencolmcille for 6km to the end of the road and the clifftop car park.

For Malin Beg Harbour, turn right just after Malinbeg Hostel. This road leads down to the harbour.

Grid refs:
Glencolmcille: G 52358 85029
Silver Strand: G 50333 79655
Malin Beg Harbour: G 49334 79918

Access to the beach at Silver Strand

37

County Donegal

Tramore, Rossbeg

When the citizens and business people of Ardara found they had been bypassed by the Wild Atlantic Way route, their roads being considered too narrow for a large volume of traffic and coaches, in true entrepreneurial style they set up their own scenic route to entice the self-drivers and cyclists. Follow the Wild Atlantic Bay signs, the icon of a crossed-out coach to show the roads will be narrow, winding and tricky. However, there is a fitting prize for the effort.

North of Ardara, take a left turn where the Wild Atlantic Bay sign guides you and pass through mature vegetation into rugged and craggy low hills. Another left turn signed to Tramore Beach and Caravan Park brings you first to Sheskinmore Nature Reserve. The reserve gate is on the roadside. There is car parking space at a lay-by and a basic map of the reserve. One of the most important reserves in Ireland,

Looking from Magheramore, County Donegal

Sheskinmore covers around 1,000 acres of marsh and sand dunes. Many different species of butterfly are to be found here, alongside many rare orchids. Wildlife is plentiful here, including badgers, foxes and otters, and, in the sky, peregrine falcons and merlin.

A 3km walk through the dunes leads to the wide expanse of the almost deserted Ballinareavy Strand. You can continue to walk from here along to Tramore Strand by veering right and following the shoreline; alternatively, return to the car at the gate to the reserve and follow the road down to a small parking area by the entrance to the camping park. The sandy track leads to the beach. Along the track, tiny mushrooms grow at the base of the sand grasses, looking like a curious miniature forest. You expect at any moment a tiny figure to walk out from behind one of these mushroom stalks and scuttle to the safety of the nearby tall reeds.

The low hummocks of white sand provide places to shelter from the wind and even near the caravan park you are soon out of sight. The beach is stunning with fine white sand and shelves very gradually. This large beach never gets crowded, the campsite is small and tucked behind the dunes and the area has a wild and exposed feel. There may be the occasional solitary walker and, near the site, children enjoying the surf. At the far end of the beach you can have the dunes and sea all to yourself.

Mushrooms in the sand dunes

Grassy dunes

Above and below: Low tide at Rossbeg Harbour, County Donegal

AT A GLANCE

SCENIC WALK | FAMILY FRIENDLY | NATURE RESERVE | CAMPING & SHORT WALK TO THE BEACH

Tramore is a lovely white sand beach with dunes behind. Walk through the nature reserve where you may see falcons hunting.

BY CAR: from Donegal town take the N56 west, then north to Ardara. Continue north of Ardara on the R261 towards Portnoo, after 6km take a left towards Rossbeg, following the Wild Atlantic Bay signs. Turn left at the sign for the camping and caravan park and follow this road. Sheskinmore Nature Reserve is accessed from a gate and stile along this road, with limited roadside parking. Climb the stile and take the 3km walk through the reserve and dunes to the large, secluded Ballinareavy Strand. For Tramore Beach continue past Sheskinmore to the end of this road and the campsite, where there is a small parking area. From here it is a short walk through to the beach. This family-run site has a couple of static caravans and room for tents or campervans.

Grid refs:
Tramore: G 68101 95833
Sheskinmore: G 68380 96387

38

County Fermanagh

Carrickreagh Jetty

Swim from this quiet jetty and island-hop in the tranquil waters of Carrickreagh Bay. The bay is sheltered between the western shore of Lower Lough Erne south-east of the 'broad lough' and Gall Island a few hundred metres to the north. Inish Fovar and Inish Lougher lie to the east. Take the extra time to climb the steep trail up through Carrickreagh Wood for fantastic views north to Donegal's Bluestack Mountains and west all the way to Sligo Bay.

The Lough Erne waterways cover a huge area in Fermanagh, with pleasure boaters, holidaymakers and kayakers all enjoying the miles of weaving rivers and lakeshore. With hundreds of islands to hop around and the great expanse of Upper Lough Erne (known locally as 'the Broad Lough') north of Devenish Island there is a wealth of places to discover. Carrickreagh is a small mooring jetty near Ely Lodge Forest on the south-western shore of Lower Lough Erne.

Surrounded by trees this is a picturesque start to a swim. An early morning dip before the touring boats begin to come in is recommended. The dark water, deep enough to dive into from the wooden jetty, is surprisingly warm as you rise up again to the surface. Tiny fish become flashes of silver as they streak away from you to stop suddenly and hang motionless, nose down tail up, as if dead, only to sprint away again when you approach. These entrancing groups of little 'spricks' play this game repeatedly: sprint – play dead – sprint. You may spy some slightly larger fish deeper below.

Diving from Carrickreagh Jetty, County Fermanagh

Moving away from the jetty, follow the depth markers which guide boats through the deep main channel. In the early morning there should be little traffic but swim along the edge of this channel to keep safely away from any passing boats. Due east from the jetty is a small island, Inish Lougher: swim the short distance across here or perhaps circumnavigate the island, approximately 1¼ miles (2km) around. Just north of Inish Lougher is the even smaller Inish Fovar. If you circumnavigate Lougher, you will see a narrow gap between the two islands almost opposite the jetty. To the north lies the smaller-still Gall Island and it is through the channel between Gall and Fovar that any visiting boats will pass.

Carrickreagh jetty is just along the river from Ely Lodge Forest. The path along the riverbank, shaded by tall trees and providing lovely views of the river, is popular with walkers. The jetty itself is a short walk along this path from the car park at Ely Lodge. The occasional boat might moor here for the night but this is one of the quiet places on the otherwise busy Erne waterways. Across the road from Carrickreagh, a steep forest track leads up to a fantastic viewpoint overlooking Lower Lough Erne all the way to the Bluestack Mountains in Donegal to the north, and Sligo Bay and the Atlantic Ocean in the west. Follow the black route indicated by waymarked posts.

AT A GLANCE

WILD CAMPING | EASY SWIM | PLENTY OF PARKING | BOATS OR CANOES

Island-hopping in the sheltered bay south-east of Upper Lough Erne (the 'Broad Lough'), a steep forest walk for superb panoramic views, all with easy access and parking close by. Canoeists will find this a great place to launch from and explore the further islands. Invest in a good map of the area if you plan a canoe tour.

There are picnic tables at the car park but no other facilities. There is easy access to the water off the wooden jetty which has a ladder at either end.

BY CAR: from Belfast take the M1 to Dungannon, then the A4 through Fivemiletown to Enniskillen. From here, head for Belleek along the A46 Shore Road. Approximately 6 miles (10km) from Enniskillen, Ely Lodge Forest car park is signed and located on the right. Alternatively, continue about 150 metres to the Carrickreagh Viewpoint Walk car park on the left. Opposite this is a path through the trees leading to the jetty.

Grid ref: H 17651 52054

39

Devenish Island

Here you can swim the short distance from the jetty at Trory Point on the mainland to Devenish Jetty to investigate the ruins of an ancient monastic settlement and climb the round tower, some 30 metres, for remarkable views. Alternatively, you can swim around the island for a different perspective, crossing the gap known as Friar's Leap where a holy man is said to have leapt across to escape the devil who was chasing him after he had broken his vows.

Lough Erne is comprised of two lakes, the Upper and Lower Loughs, which are joined by a meandering watercourse. Popular with all kinds of water-sports enthusiasts, this inland waterway, stretching from Belleek in the north-west to Belturbet in the

Trory Point Jetty, with Devenish Island in the background, County Fermanagh

south-east, is studded with islands. For the swimmer there are many spots, either from the riverbanks or along Upper Lough Erne, known as the 'Broad Lough'. Devenish Island, with its religious ruins and sheltered waters, makes for one of the best swimming spots close to Enniskillen.

With its round tower standing proud on the soft green mound of grass the temptation is to simply cross the short stretch of water by ferry onto Devenish like any other tourist but a swim to circumnavigate the island provides a unique perspective.

Plunging in from the wooden jetty at Trory, you may be pleasantly surprised by the warmth of the water. Shallow water here warms quickly during the summer months and the soft peaty base of the lough holds the heat. Travelling anticlockwise around the island, take a swim-tour through misadventure and local history.

Devenish Island was a monastic site founded in the sixth century by St Molaise and, during its history, has been raided by Vikings, burned, and flourished as a parish. The 2km-long island takes its name from the Irish: *Daimhinis*, meaning 'Ox Island'.

Devenish Island with its monastic round tower, church and cloister, County Fermanagh

The earliest ruins on the island are from the twelfth century: St Molaise's House, a small church and the striking round tower. St Mary's Augustinian Priory on the hilltop has a church, tower and cloister dating from the mid-fifteenth/sixteenth century and in the graveyard stands an intricately carved stone cross, also from the fifteenth century.

Rounding the southern end of the island, cross Friar's Leap, a stretch of water between Devenish and a small islet just off the mainland. From here, round the south of the island and come to Devenish Jetty. A short way north is Trory Jetty, our starting point.

Running north/south and at 1¼ miles (2km) long and ⅔ mile (1km) wide, this circumnavigation is a long swim. There is, however, the option of taking a short swim from Trory Jetty south to Devenish Jetty to explore the island. Take a dry bag for clothing or wear a wetsuit and booties.

Lough Erne waterways are full of places to swim but be aware that the area is very popular for fishing and boating so make yourself highly visible and keep out of the deeper channels unless accompanied by a canoe or kayak. Devenish is one of the more sheltered bays with less boat traffic.

AT A GLANCE

ISLAND SWIM | EASY ACCESS | SOME BOATS

Either circumnavigate the island, approximately a 3-mile (5km) swim, or take the short jaunt from Trory Point Jetty to Devenish Jetty, approximately 800 metres south and visible from Trory.

BY CAR: from Belfast, take the M1 West. Near Dungannon, the road becomes the A4. Follow it to Ballgawley Roundabout and continue on the A4 through Augher, Clogher and Fivemiletown into Enniskillen. Turn right onto the A32 towards Irvinestown, for 2 miles (3km). Just before the roundabout at Trory, turn left at the filling station onto a minor road. after ¾ mile (1.2km) take the left fork in the road.

Grid ref: H 22644 47735

40

County Donegal

Kinnagoe, Inishowen Peninsula

The Inishowen 100 scenic route passes Kinnagoe Bay with its deep golden sands and three separate beaches, the first of which is claimed by many to be the most beautiful beach in Ireland. Here divers regularly come to seek artefacts from the wreck of the Armada ship *La Trinidad Valencera*, which was lost in 1588. The wreck was discovered in 1971.

The first view of the stunning beach from the top of the hill on this scenic route will make your heart beat faster with anticipation. The road drops steeply down as you weave around each corner, pulling into the widened lay-bys when you meet another vehicle coming back up, impatient to reach your destination. At the shore there is a large tarmacked parking area. The beach stretches out to the right with sand so deep and soft you sink to your ankles. Kick off your shoes and wade through the golden swamp on this popular beach where, in the summer, some families will pitch their tents and remain here for weeks on end.

Rock formation at Kinnagoe

Foaming stream at Kinnagoe

The largest of Kinnagoe's three beaches on the Inishowen Peninsula, County Donegal

Brown crab at Kinnagoe

Beach at Kinnagoe

The beach is large so there is plenty of space for all. Swim in the clear waters and snorkel around the rocks in search of Armada treasure but, if you want more privacy, walk the length of the strand to a narrow track that climbs up and over the rocks to a second, quieter, bay. Few come this far so you may well have this beach to yourself. The sand is still deep and soft. Search for shells washed up on shore and enjoy the solitude. Halfway along this bay an area of long grass bridges the gap between the foliage-dense hillside and the sand; a river runs out to the sea. Press through this thick grass upstream a few hundred metres to a small waterfall and a shallow bathing pool. The dark water spilling over the rocks fizzles as it is aerated, a creamy-white foam pouring into an inky pool.

At the far end of this bay there is another track up and over the rocks leading into a third, even more secluded bay. Here you can be alone with only the wheeling birds and the swish of the sea for company. Very few venture this far and so it is a quiet spot for those inclined to skinny-dip.

AT A GLANCE

SCENIC WALK | FAMILY FRIENDLY | BEACH CAMPING

Sink ankle deep in the soft sands of the three strands at Kinnagoe Bay, on the north-eastern shore of the Inishowen Peninsula, approximately 10km from Moville. Camp on the first and most popular beach or cross the strand and follow a narrow track over the rocks to the second, quieter, bay; an even more secluded third cove lies over a second headland, about twenty minutes' walk away from the first beach.

BY CAR: from Derry/Londonderry city, take the A2 north, then follow the R238 along the shore of Lough Foyle to Moville. The R238 sweeps away from the shoreline here. Look for the left turn onto the Inishowen 100 towards Ballybane and Kinnagoe. The beach is signed down a long, narrow and winding road to car parking at the bottom.

Grid ref: C 62832 46114

41

County Donegal

Dunagree Point, Inishowen Peninsula

The rugged rock formation and man-made bridge lead to a fascinating swim at Stroove Beach, Dunagree Point, County Donegal

Follow the road out of Moville towards Inishowen Head and stop at almost any hole in the hedge to park your car or bike on the roadside. Take a peek through that gap and you will probably find a cove or tiny beach, completely deserted. If not, and it is solitude you want, there are plenty more to explore. With a coastal walk, rocks to dive from and two beaches at which to swim, Dunagree is a gem with the added charm of having camping space on either of the two beaches. With the Atlantic swell washing into this little bay one can play in the surf or swim out beyond the breakers. One can even venture around the lighthouse to the smaller beach, finish the day with a barbeque and listen to the gentle lull of the waves as evening light descends.

The Arch, which leads to St Columba's Cove near Dunagree Point, County Donegal

Dunagree Lighthouse sits in private gardens flanked by two beaches: the first, small and sheltered with soft white sand quickly shelving into deep water, tends to be deserted, visitors preferring the handy car parking of the second larger beach. The car park is basic, a rectangle of tarmac with two Portaloos to the side. A lifeguard's hut perches on the dune above the beach. There is a quaint old-fashionedness about it all. The lighthouse sits above the dunes to the right of the bay and, to the left, the rough and craggy rocks carry an old concrete bridge which beckons to the explorer. This bridge once led to a diving board, long since gone.

From these rocks there is a shoreline track that leads around to 'the Arch', which locals promise you will know when you see it, and you will. Follow the rough track from

Evening swim at Dunagree Point

the beach, passing several inlets and rocky coves where one could swim, but continue to the Arch, which is a special, secret place.

The track is indeed rough and trainers rather than sandals are recommended for pushing through the tall forest of bracken that seems determined to trip the unwary with broken strands trailing across the path. Wet leaves sweep across your legs as you thread your way along this coastal trail. Soon the bracken clears and views of the craggy Donegal coast are revealed again.

At each inlet you may think 'is this it?' but no, not secluded enough, not romantic enough, so follow the path as it curves on, around the next corner, over the next rise. Again push through tall bracken until the path drops back down onto the shore, climb over the occasional large rock and then you will see it: there is no doubt as here, just as the path turns the corner, a high cliff juts out from the shore into the sea, blocking the path save for a low doorway through the wall of rock: the Arch. Step through this archway into the ancient amphitheatre of St Columba's Cove. At low tide the strange-shaped rocks take on the form of all sorts of creatures – dolphins and mermaids waiting for the tide to return, great swathes of curving tails sitting silently, the black rocks gleaming with the last traces of the outgoing tide. This quiet place could awaken wonders of the imagination...

AT A GLANCE

BEACH CAMPING | SCENIC WALK | FAMILY FRIENDLY

Beach camping, a rugged coastal path and swimming as the sun goes down on either of the two beaches. Camping is possible on either beach: the small beach is accessed through a field where a little byre houses a few cattle, fenced off from the strand. Pitch up anywhere along this shoreline above the high-water mark. The larger beach might be preferable, keeping closer to the Portaloos. To the left of the track that leads from the car park onto the sand a low wall of rock provides shelter from wind and prying eyes.

BY CAR: from Derry/Londonderry city take the A2 to Muff and then the R238 along the shores of Lough Foyle, through Moville. From there, take the R241 through Greencastle towards Stroove. Dunagree is the last beach before the road loops back on itself at Inishowen Head.

Grid ref: C 68255 42693

County Antrim

Dunseverick Harbour and Slough

Climb the rocks to plunge from various heights into this little-known gem on the north coast. The Slough at Dunseverick is a cleft cut in the rocks, forming a deep inlet perfect for jumping and diving, narrow and sheltered from the North Atlantic. The black rocks provide plenty of diving platforms.

On the coast road between Ballintoy and Bushmills, Dunseverick could easily be missed but take the single-track road off towards the shore, signed for Dunseverick Harbour, and park along the verge. The Slough is found by climbing over the wooden stile on the roadside, which leads through a field scattered with granite rocks and gorse (whin) ablaze with bright yellow flowers from spring. The grass gives way to more rocks until one stumbles across the narrow cleft in the rocks, sheltered from the worst of the Atlantic swell. This deep, narrow inlet has rocks of varying heights from which

Diving into an inflatable ring at the Slough, with a view towards Dunserverick Harbour, County Antrim

to plunge. On one side, small patches of sand provide natural picnic sites sheltered from the breeze between the large rocks. On the other side, the black stone absorbs the sun's rays and hours can be spent clambering, jumping and diving, using the heat from the rocks to warm oneself. The water is clear and very deep and there are plenty of sheltered nooks in which to settle out of the wind.

Here, young men aim to dive through the centre of a giant inflatable ring from a height while others lounge on neon bright lilos, shouting encouragement; a mix of wetsuited and swimsuited explorers challenge themselves to ever higher jumps and dives.

For those who want a longer swim, the picturesque Dunseverick Harbour at the end of the narrow road is a good place to park. The pretty, whitewashed harbourmaster's cottage is still manned by a caretaker during the summer months and the current

caretaker has a wealth of stories to tell. From here, walk into crystal-clear waters between the two jetties and marvel at the variety of colours of the kelp and other seaweeds as large fish cruise beneath, oblivious to your presence, the perfect spot for snorkelling.

It is possible to swim from here to the Slough: swim out from the harbour and turn left between the two large rocks. Follow the shoreline to the Slough about 750 metres away. The swell of the North Atlantic gives this the feeling of a wild adventure swim, even with no breakers, the gentle swell in the water can seem like the sea is breathing quietly but with immense underlying power.

Follow the craggy coastline past rocky outcrops, which drop steeply into depths full of life. Limpets cling to the rocks, anemones dance in the sway of the current and tiny crabs bustle about as fish weave in and out of the kelp forest deep below. Look out for the entrance to the Slough where the water turns to glass as you glide into the sheltered inlet. Allow time for jumping and diving before heading back into the North Sea on the return journey to the harbour.

From the harbour, take the coastal path between the Causeway and Carrick-a-Rede, or make the short walk up to Dunseverick Castle, a key site in ancient Ireland, which St Patrick visited many times and to where one of the royal roads from Tara is said to have run.

AT A GLANCE

FAMILY FRIENDLY | SNORKELLING | ROCK-POOLS | JUMPING WITH CARE | POPULAR/BUSY | ROCKS & HAZARDS

The Slough at Dunseverick provides a sheltered inlet for lazing away long summer days: jumping, diving, plunging and picnicking. Strong swimmers may want to swim from the petite Dunseverick Harbour along the rugged coastline and into the shelter of the Slough. This is for strong, competent swimmers as, while it is not a long swim, the tides here are formidable. The Slough, though, is suitable for many levels of swimmer. The North Atlantic is cold with powerful swells, so know your limitations and always swim safe.

Car parking and public toilets at the harbour. No camping.

BY CAR: from Belfast, travel north on the M2 for 14.9 miles (24km). At junction 1 take the A26 towards Antrim/Ballymena/Coleraine. Continue north towards Ballymena/Coleraine. At the roundabout take the third exit onto the A26, travel 7 miles (11km) and at the roundabout take the third exit onto the A36 towards Coleraine/Ballymena/Larne. Continue onto the M2 then merge onto the A26. After 4.8 miles (7.7km) turn right onto the A44 towards Ballycastle and drive a further 13.8 miles (22km) to Ballycastle. From Ballycastle, drive west on the B15 coast road to Ballintoy. Follow the signpost for the Giant's Causeway onto the B146, and then follow the signpost to Dunseverick Harbour. Park on the roadside by the wooden stile and walk over the field to the Slough (five minutes). Alternatively, Dunseverick Harbour at the end of this single-track road has a car park and toilets. From here, scramble up to Dunseverick Castle or join the coastal path from the Giant's Causeway to Ballintoy Harbour.

BY BUS: the Causeway Rambler Bus runs during summer between Bushmills and Carrick-a-rede.

Grid refs:
Dunseverick Harbour: C 99979 44510
The Slough: C 99679 44529

43

Larrybane Bay and Carrick-a-Rede Rope Bridge

Carrick-a-Rede Rope Bridge, County Antrim

Swim in clear turquoise waters across Larrybane Bay past rugged white cliffs with great boulders spilling into the sea to the tiny island of Carrick-a-Rede. Swim under the narrow rope bridge high above and move into the deeper waters to the east of the island, the cliffs rising up all around.

A rough track curves down from the old quarry below the main car park at Carrick-a-Rede and the popular path leading to the rope bridge spanning the chasm between the mainland and the island. As you turn the corner the first views of Sheep Island appear to the west, where strong currents swirl the water into eddies. A line of calm water can be clearly seen between here and the sheltered Larrybane Bay, stretching east towards the island, the rope bridge just visible. On the shore, white chalky cliffs housing wind-carved chasms stretch up from the huge boulders which in turn melt into pale sand beneath the turquoise sea. Along the shore are perfect white rounded

Carrick-a-Rede Rope Bridge (below) and Larrybane Bay (facing page), County Antrim

pebbles; the high grass-topped island, tethered to the mainland by the rope-bridge, is a picturesque scene.

Almost 9 miles (14km) from the Giant's Causeway, Carrick-a-Rede island sits only a short distance from the shore but, with high cliffs making it inaccessible to walk to, fishermen have built bridges across to its rich salmon fishing for over 350 years. Now managed by the National Trust, in the summer the rope bridge draws thousands of visitors whose squeals of fear and laughter echo around the bay as they carefully cross to the island; some turn back, daunted by the vertiginous crossing.

For swimmers the opportunity to view the bridge from a different angle is the reward of a scramble over the rocks at Larrybane, followed by the long swim across the bay. Explore the caves beneath the island, which were once used as shelter in stormy weather by boatbuilders.

In fair weather the swim across is pleasant, a good 1 mile (2km) round trip with the sun lighting up the clear, shallow waters. The floor of the bay is sandy and a small beach at the base of the island reveals the first shallow cave. From this beach, go around to the narrow gap between the island and shore, swimming beneath the rope bridge. At certain times the route may even be shallow enough to walk, dipping and undulating in the soft sand like the rubber floor in a fairground funhouse.

On the far side of the bridge, great black cliffs soar upwards and the shallow caves amplify the sound of the waves, turning the smallest swell into a low, deep boom. These waters are where the salmon were corralled by the fishermen. On the island, a set of steep steps leads down from the tiny fisherman's cottage, past a broken and rusting winch, a remnant of the old salmon fishery, to the waters' edge.

Return under the bridge, all the way back across this picturesque bay to climb out and scramble back up over the rocks.

AT A GLANCE

SCENIC WALK | SECLUDED | SEA CAVES | DIFFICULT PATH | ADVENTURE SWIM | ROCKS AND HAZARDS

From Larrybane Bay, swim beneath the Carrick-a-Rede Rope Bridge to the old salmon fisheries. Explore the caves beneath the island. This is an advanced swim for the experienced open-water swimmer. Although not difficult it requires knowledge both of the swimmer's limitations and of the local tides.

It is wise to avoid the bay to the west of Sheep Island as here the currents are much stronger and the eddies can be powerful.

BY CAR: this is a 1 hour 15 minute drive from Belfast and 10 minutes from the Giant's Causeway. From Belfast take the M2 north through Ballymena, then the A26, turning onto the A44 to Ballycastle. Take the B15 coast road towards Ballintoy and Carrick-a-Rede.

Travelling from Bushmills take the B15 for about 4 miles (7km) and follow the signs to Carrick-a-Rede Rope Bridge, a National Trust site.

Drive through the main car park and down to the overspill car park in the Quarry. Leave the car here and follow the track on foot to the shore. Sandals are recommended.

BY BUS: the Ulster Bus Causeway Rambler service runs between Bushmills and Carrick-a-Rede during the summer. The no. 252 is a circular route through the Antrim Glens from Belfast: check with Ulster Bus for timetables.

Grid ref: D 06106 44854

44

County Antrim

Portmuck, Island Magee

North of Belfast city and through the ancient town of Carrickfergus along the coast road, take a side trip to the pretty Island Magee. Quiet country roads and breathtaking scenery are the offerings of this tiny peninsula, perfect for cyclists, with good hill climbs and unparalleled views across the North Channel. Once a haven for smugglers, Portmuck is now a serene sight. Whitewashed cottages sit high on the cliffs, overlooking the old-fashioned harbour. Many who own the holiday cottages have spent their summers here since childhood so there is a great family atmosphere. One feels as though any of the neighbours would invite you in for a cup of tea.

Fishermen and swimmers share the harbour at Portmuck, Island Magee, County Antrim

The White Rocks at Portmuck

The harbour is sheltered on both sides from the battering of the North Channel by tall cliffs and this natural cove is further protected from the strong tides by the nearby Isle of Muck, or Pig Island. Entering the water from the public slipway and swimming out past the harbour walls one feels transported back to a simpler time. The wall juts out from the rugged coastline as you swim across the cove beneath the vintage cottages perched above on the cliffs, while cormorants and oystercatchers bob unconcerned alongside.

The water is silky as it glides over your skin. As the shock of cold wears off, one feels connected to the landscape, submerged in it, the slight movement of the sea hinting at the power in the tide that the calm surface belies. As one returns to the harbour, the shallower water seems a little warmer.

There are several walks up over the cliffs from the harbour that provide terrific views across to Scotland. The northern route is through the swing gate to the left: follow the path up, cross a stile and open fields to the boundary and return by the same route. The southern route starts at the harbour steps: climb these to follow the path down more steps to the rocky shore. Turn right and carry on until you reach the tombolo across to Pig Island.

Or travel to the south of Portmuck Harbour to visit the Victorian cliff paths of the Gobbins, named after the terrifying giant Gobbin Saor who, in days of legend, lived in these basalt cliffs. Built in 1909, a triumph of Victorian engineering, this 2-mile (3km) path of steps, bridges and tunnels spans waterfalls and plunges down almost 60 metres to the Irish Sea. After years of neglect, extensive works were carried out to repair the pathways to their former glory. Reopened in summer 2015, the path has superb walkways and bridges along the cliff side and guided tours are run throughout the season.

Nearby, Brown's Bay is a long, wide strand, with good parking. Ideal for longer training swims for both open-water swimmers and triathletes, Brown's is a 300-metre-long beach with rocks and loose boulders around the edge. The relative remoteness of this site gives it a real 'away-from-it-all' feel and in clear weather one can see five headlands all the way up the Antrim coast. A superb place for stretching out on a longer swim or enjoying a picnic; a good place for an evening swim.

AT A GLANCE

SCENIC WALK | FAMILY FRIENDLY | BOATS OR CANOES | POPULAR | JUMPING WITH CARE

Portmuck Harbour is well sheltered and provides a beautiful swimming area but be aware of strong tides outside the harbour and around Pig Island where it is not recommended to swim. The quiet harbour has good car parking and toilet facilities.

BY CAR: travelling north from Belfast city on the A2 towards Larne, turn right onto the B90 then take the B150, following the signs to Portmuck. The road to the harbour is narrow, winding and steep and the final hill affords a wonderful view across to Pig Island.

Grid refs:
Portmuck Harbour: D 46008 02353
Brown's Bay Beach: D 43630 02870

45

County Down

Benderg Bay and Lecale Way

Two for one at this sheltered coastline: first, walk through the grasslands of Killard Nature Reserve to Benderg Beach, home to sand martins and seals. Perfect on a sunny day for swimming, picnicking and investigating the rock pools. The more adventurous will enjoy walking the Lecale Way shoreline track from Ballyhornan, past Gunn's Island and on to the cleft in the rocks at Benboy Hill for jumping and diving.

Kayakers take a break and a dip in one of the Lecale Way's many inlets, County Down

Veiw of beach and Gunn's Island from Ballyhornan, Lecale Way, County Down

From the small town of Strangford, the Lecale Way follows the County Down coastline for 31 miles (50km) along quiet roads, past beaches and on coastal paths, all the way to the ancient dune system of Murlough Bay, Ireland's first nature reserve.

South of Strangford and just outside the mouth of Strangford Lough lies Killard Nature Reserve and the secluded Benderg Bay. This superb strand stretches just over half a kilometre from the rocks of Killard Point to the sand cliffs and farmland that separate Benderg from its more popular neighbour, Ballyhornan Beach.

You may see seals lounging at Mill Quarter Bay, where the strength of Strangford Lough's tidal run creates whirlpools and the tidal turbine generates electric power from the swift-moving water. This is not the place to swim, however: leave it to the seals. A twenty-minute walk from here through the orchid-filled grasslands of the nature reserve leads to Benderg. Tucked away behind Killard Point, the beach is out of the way of Strangford's powerful tidal race and you can swim in crystal-clear shallow waters as sand martins swoop from the cliffs across the bay. The rocks at the left of the beach are teeming with life, including young seals hunting for crab among the seaweed.

One can spend a lazy day picnicking and swimming before returning to the car, back across the meadow-like grassland. Alternatively, one can scramble the rough coastline from here south to Ballyhornan Beach, the more popular strand. At the far

end of Ballyhornan a narrow trail leads along the Lecale Way coastal path eventually coming to Ardglass Village. The footpath runs along the foreshore, past tiny coves where sand and shale has been washed in between banks of rocks to form intimate bays. Approximately half an hour's walk along this path from the beach brings you to a superb inlet for jumping and diving. The path rises steeply up to a rickety wooden stile and then a sweeping curve above the inlet. Access to the water is by scrambling down the steep grass banks, then onto the rocks on either side of this inlet. Take care climbing down to this deep and appealing spot, which is great for jumping. Watch the tides to ensure you can climb out again. This is one for strong swimmers.

Benderg Bay, looking towards Gunn's Island and the Mourne Mountains, Lecale Way
Facing page: Jumping in Lecale Way's many inlets, County Down

Strangford is the largest sea lough in the British Isles and, at the narrow channel between Strangford and Portaferry, 400 million tonnes of water flow in and out of the lough each day creating massive currents and whirlpools. Benderg is sheltered from these strong currents as it curves away from the mouth of the lough.

AT A GLANCE

SCENIC WALK | FAMILY FRIENDLY | SECLUDED | SNORKELLING | ROCK POOLS |
ADVENTURE SWIM

Benderg Bay is a secluded beach of pale sand, stretching half a kilometre behind Killard Nature Reserve. This gently shelving bay provides a great swim or dip, and is home to sand martins and seals.

Alternatively, walk the Lecale Way for quiet inlets and coves for the excitement of a great wild swim. A pleasant walk is followed by a rock climb and swim, great for jumping and exploring. Keep a good eye on water levels to ensure a safe exit.

From Strangford take the car ferry to Portaferry to witness the strong currents and visit the aquarium with its orphan seals and touch tanks for a great family day out.

BY CAR: take the A2 Shore Road out of Strangford. At Kilclief veer left towards Mill Quarter Bay. Park at the roadside lay-by from where signs point to the track leading into Killard Nature Reserve. Follow the path past the mouth of Strangford Lough. The rough track cuts through farmland and on to Benderg Bay. Roadside parking, no facilities, twenty-minute walk to beach.

Grid refs:
Benderg Bay: J 60722 43067
Lecale Way: J 58738 40207
Start of coastal path: J 59251 41810

46

County Down

Janet's Rock, Ballymartin

Seaside scene at Janet's Rock, Ballymartin, County Down

Banks of rock stretching into the sea create an intimate sandy cove. Swim in the crystal-clear water of the sheltered bay with a myriad of seaweed colours on the rocky floor where fish hide in crevasses and tiny crabs scuttle. Then climb barefoot and explore the rock pools to the left of the cove. Search for tiny sea creatures or glide underwater through a narrow gap in the rocks from one pool into another.

The A2 coastal road from Newcastle in County Down, travelling south, takes one through the small towns of Ballymartin and Kilkeel all the way into Carlingford Lough and the pretty village of Rostrevor. With the Mourne Mountains rising up to one side and the road hugging the coast, there are many narrow lanes leading down to the shore where hidden beaches, known only to locals, provide some superb swimming.

At Ballymartin, halfway between Annalong and Kilkeel, Janet's Rock is easy to find, and has a bus stop very close to the top of the laneway.

The steep, rough track drops down from the road to the shore revealing the small cove created by two banks of rock jutting out from the shoreline strand. It is a perfect contained bathing area. The rocky outcrop to the left of the sandy beach gives its name to the spot – Janet's Rock – and forms one wall sheltering the bay from the open sea. To the right a low bank of boulders creates the second wall and within these two outcrops the water is clear and calm. The bay quickly gets to a good depth for swimming. In the shallows you may have to step over a few rocks before you get to the deep water.

Janet's Rock, to the left of the bay, has pools to explore, some large enough to swim in, and at the point farthest out, when the tide is high, one can dive from these rocks into the bay.

Several lobster pots lie moored a little way outside the cove and seals are often seen here. It has been known as a place where seals will form groups and hunt together, chasing the fish and corralling them in the small bay.

A world away from the busy strand at Cranfield, south of Kilkeel, Janet's Rock will often be entirely deserted, with perhaps just the occasional fisherman heading out to check his lobster pots.

Above and facing page: swimmers at Janet's Rock, Ballymartin, County Down

AT A GLANCE

FAMILY FRIENDLY | SECLUDED | ROCK POOLS | JUMPING WITH CARE

A delightful bay, with a few locals during the summer. Scramble over rocks and through small rock pools, then dive back into the sheltered bay to swim. This little bay is a secret gem of a place, which you may have completely to yourself.

From here walk south along the strand towards Ballymartin where another path will bring you back up alongside a small stream to the road. In nearby Kilkeel check out Seascope NI beside the harbour, a lobster and marine hatchery which is open to the public.

No facilities but very close to Ballymartin.

BY CAR: from Newry: take the A2 to Warrenpoint and continue along the coast through Rostrevor and Kilkeel. Ballymartin is approximately 3 miles (5km) north-east of Kilkeel, heading towards Annalong. Janet's Rock is on the Annalong side of Ballymartin village.

Just beyond the village proper a roadside bus stop opposite several houses marks the stony laneway. Park in the lay-by, walk approximately 50 yards along the road to the lane down to shore. The lane is rough and although there is room to turn and park at the bottom it would be worth walking first. Take care driving onto the soft sand as it is easy to get a car stuck!

BY BUS: Translink route no. 37 runs between Newcastle and Kilkeel.

Grid ref: J 35155 17209

Counties Cavan/Monaghan

Dromore River, Cootehill

Skip from county to county, from Cavan into Monaghan and back again, as you front crawl or breast stroke along the Dromore River towards Drumlona Lough, weaving back and forth across the county border as it cuts down the centre of the river. River swims close to towns are not something I would usually recommend, but here in the heart of the lakelands the Dromore River is an absolute gem. Tall reeds line the riverbank as the swimmer quietly meanders along.

The Dromore River, which runs through Cootehill, County Cavan/Monaghan border

Drying off after a swim, Cootehill

Cootehill has its fair share of the 365 loughs of Cavan, nestled between the rivers Dromore and Annalee and, with 26 lakes within a 16km radius, ranging from the large Lough Sillan in the south to the small but beautiful Annamakerrig in the north, it is little wonder this area has been a favourite haunt for artists, writers, poets and playwrights, including Percy French and Seamus Heaney.

Along the shores of the river, teenagers lounge in small boats at the waters' edge, so deep in conversation they hardly notice as you breast stroke by. Any one of these teens may follow in the footsteps of artists and be inspired to write or create by simply taking the time to relax and drift in the flow of the stream.

From Cootehill town centre, take the road out of town towards Dartry. Approaching the border between Cavan and Monaghan along this road you will cross an old bridge.

Look for the small car park on the right. Park here. Either swim from the grassy bank in shallow waters at the bridge or walk a little distance along the wooded pathway. Every so often a wooden boardwalk, only two planks wide, juts out from the path to a little jetty. Anglers use these stands and there is the occasional small boat tucked into the tall reeds. The opposite bank leads into Bellamont Forest, a 1,000-acre estate with woodlands and Bellamont House, the first Palladian villa built in Ireland. It was built by the Cootes, who also founded the town of Coote Hill, which, by the 1800s, was a prosperous linen town.

Swimming is actively encouraged around Cootehill and few will bat an eye at a swimmer. During the summer water-safety classes are run here.

Have a quick dip or venture as far along the river as you wish. The flow is gentle and not too fast. If in any doubt of your swimming strength, first swim upstream to have the benefit of the flow helping you on the return journey. This is always a good way to get a feel of how strong the flow is and may help you decide how far you are willing to swim each time.

AT A GLANCE

RIVER SWIMMING, EITHER DIP OR JOURNEY | LOCAL GROUPS | SCENIC WALKS NEARBY

Enjoy a meandering river swim, passing small fishing stands and skipping from one county to the other as you make your way along this border waterway. Popular with swimmers during the summer and running water-safety lessons for children, there is still solitude to be found by venturing further downriver where the fishing jetties provide perfect access for the swimmer (just remember which stand you left your gear at).

BY CAR: From Monaghan town take the N54, turning onto the R188 towards Cootehill. Park at New Bridge just before you cross the Dromore River.

Cootehill is 16km north-east of Cavan and 1¼ hours from Dublin, take the M3 Navan road to Kells then N3 towards Cavan, travel through Virginia and take the R165 then R168 to Cootehill.

BY BUS: Bus Éireann has services from both Cavan and Monaghan.

Grid ref: H 59741 15153

County Cavan

Lough Ramor

Tractor surfing at Lough Ramor, Virginia, County Cavan

There are 365 loughs in County Cavan, one for each day of the year: how to choose, then, where to swim? My advice, check out Lough Ramor: it has camping on the lakeshore, rowboats for hire and islands to swim out to and explore, all enhanced by the landowner, Tommy Conaty who will regale you with stories of the area. Book a pitch on this simple campsite and enjoy the tranquil setting looking across the lough to Virginia town.

On the approach to Virginia the view of the lake opens up and one's heart begins to beat a little faster. There is something old fashioned about the small towns of Ireland: is it the lack of conglomerate stores or the abundance of independents? Is it the attitude of the inhabitants? All seems just a little more relaxed, a little eccentric. Whatever the reason, it encourages a spirit of exploration and I, for one, am less inclined to worry if someone thinks me silly. This childlike (or childish) feeling led me to agreeing to hop on the back of a tractor in only my swimsuit and be driven across the shallow sandbank towards the nearest island. Practising my surfing stance on the grass topper, which only minutes earlier had been zipping over the field in preparation for the first influx of campers due in the next few weeks, I heard Tommy, the farmer and landowner, call back, 'I must be ready for the mad-house! Who'd have thought I'd have a mermaid on the back of ma tractor?'

The swimming here is lovely, a gently shelving lake with thirty-two islands to explore, some just a short swim from the campsite. The town of Virginia is approximately 2.5km across the lough and if you want to swim the full length of the lough it is nearly 5km long. With no jet-skis allowed, this is an ideal place for swimmers and kayakers.

The campsite is basic and right on the water's edge, a 'Wild Camping' sign on the locked gate has a contact number: phone Tommy for the access code. Tommy runs a tight ship here: he doesn't mind who comes, whether they want to fish or boat (he also hires out rowboats) or swim, as long they leave the place as they found it. He has no tolerance for rubbish, and will photograph the evidence if any is left. The result is a splendid, pristine field: picnic tables dot the shoreline, birds skim across the surface

View from slipway of Lough Ramor, Virginia, County Cavan

of the water as fish leap, and three small boats lean on the gravel shore, ready for takers.

After a short walk across the field, Tommy showed me the small bay where every summer around 150 local schoolchildren come for lessons in swimming and life-saving skills, and for barbeques and picnics. The Guides and Scouts troops are regulars along with fishermen and holidaymakers from Europe.

The facilities are basic: there are toilets and showers at the house at the top of the lane; at busy periods, portable toilets are put in place also. Other than that, it is wild camping.

No bonfires are allowed, although Tommy does not mind a small campfire, saying, 'there's nothing nicer on a summer evening than to make a circle of stones and sit around a fire, chatting and singing as the sun goes down over the lake.' Just don't leave any bottles or cans.

Relaxing dip in Lough Ramor, Virginia

AT A GLANCE

LAKESIDE CAMPING | ISLAND SWIMS | FRIENDLY ATMOSPHERE

A basic lakeside campsite with a shallow inlet and a wide slipway, from where one can swim out to several islands or even swim across the lake to Virginia town. The campsite is 6km from Virginia and Oldcastle on the south bank of Lough Ramor – or a 2.5km swim across from the slipway. There are plenty of shops, pubs, restaurants and coffee shops in the towns.

See www.loughramorcamping.com for charges and other information.

BY CAR: 85km north-west of Dublin, Virginia is on the N3. Go through the centre of town on the R194, turn left onto the R195, then look for signs to Lough Ramor Wild Camping on the left. The laneway leads to two small cottages and a locked gate. Call the mobile number on the sign for the access code. You can drive down to the lakeshore where there is parking either on the gravel slipway or in the field.

Grid ref: N 57807 86029

Salterstown Pier, Annagassan

Salterstown Pier is the locals' gathering place, the place to swim and picnic and while away lazy summer days. Those in the know say it is the best spot hereabouts. The low pier wall serves both as a windbreak and buffet table, laden with fruits and snacks to keep the revellers going. Swimsuits and towels lie stretched out to dry and from barbeques the aroma of sausages wafts across Dundalk Bay, with the backdrop of the Cooley Mountains across the bay and the Mournes hazy in the distance.

Whether the tide is in or out, the pier provides a perfect walkway into the clear water, free from the pebbles on the seabed. As barefoot children run back and forth, teenagers dive into the deeper water and search for crabs while other swimmers tour the length of the shore as far as they wish. The water is clear here and, although there is little beach to speak of, swimming from the pier creates a sense of adventure not to

Previous spread and below: View towards the Cooley and Mourne Mountains from Salterstown Pier at Annagassan, County Louth

be found so easily at the nearby and popular beaches of Annagassan and Clogherhead.

After a full day's swimming, diving, exploring and admiring the views of the mountains, take the shore road north past Annagassan Beach and drive approximately 10km to the small town of Blackrock. With a lively seaside-resort feel, it is a world away from Salterstown Pier. Stop at Café Acqua for an ice cream as the sun goes down and your body tingles with the memory of your swim.

AT A GLANCE

FAMILY FRIENDLY | GOOD ACCESS FOR KAYAKS

Salterstown Pier is a long, narrow slipway reaching out into Dundalk Bay; the shore around it is stony and at low tide the sand is revealed. Walk or swim along the coast, north towards Annagasssan or south towards Dunany Point. Salterstown lies south of Dundalk and only 4km from Annagassan, which has a lovely long strand.

BY CAR: from Dundalk take the R132 south towards Castlebellingham, then the R166 to Annagassan. At the southern end of Annagasssan Beach turn left onto the scenic route along the shore towards Dunany Point. This quiet country road is perfect for a coastal cycle, past white stone cottages.

Alternatively, take the M1 to Junction 15 at Castlebellingham, then the R166 to Annagassan.

BY BUS: Bus Éireann has a service from Dundalk to Annagassan. Salterstown Pier is on the Coast Road, almost 3.5km from Annagassan. Walk south-east along the beachside R166 Strand Road, approximately 1.4km to a fork where the road sweeps to the right. Follow the left-hand fork onto Coast Road. Salterstown Pier is a further 1.8km. The beach at Annagassan is an alternative if you do not wish to walk the country roads.

Grid ref: O 11794 93347

County Louth

Clogherhead and Port Oriel

With countryside to rival any on the west coast of Ireland, Clogherhead has a popular beach. Chalets line the rise behind the strand, making the most of their sea view. The gently shelving beach gradually fills as families come out to enjoy the sun, with all, including the family dog, racing into the waves before heading back up the beach for breakfast. Families here take pride in their chalet life during the summer months and many come back generation after generation to this prized spot.

Below and following page: View southward along the beach at Clogherhead, County Louth

Taking the path from the beach there is a pleasant walk from the village along the sea cliffs into picturesque Port Oriel Harbour. 'Be guided by the Dancing Starfish,' the locals say. This grassy track passes up over the headland, full of places to scramble and explore. Craggy inlets topped with mauve clover flowerheads and white daisies lead down into deep gorges. Climb down one of these gorges to plunge in and, as you swim around the rock face, discover what remains of Red Man's Cave, almost inaccessible now after decades of marine erosion.

There are several gory tales as to how this place got its name: one is set during the Cromwellian wars of 1649, which tells of Cromwell's soldiers having put to death a number of Catholic priests here. Until recently the cave was painted red to commemorate this event, but time and the ravages of the sea have worn it away almost completely.

Another story tells of a Spanish ship's crew, many of whom had died of scurvy during their voyage to these shores. The remaining six and their captain camped at the cave but each night another man would die, until only three crew and the captain were left. Suspecting their captain of foul play, these last few men cut off his head and placed it in the cave. Legend says that at night a spectral man can be seen walking around the area, singing and whistling.

Moving back into the bright sunlight washes away the shivers of ghost stories. Follow the rocky coastline further and you will soon come to the harbour. The metal sculpture of a starfish is a happy sight, waving to welcome visitors to Port Oriel as he dances along the harbour wall. Call in at Fisherman's Catch for fresh seafood which has travelled all of 50 metres from the boat to the fishmongers' shelves.

AT A GLANCE

SCENIC WALK | LIFEGUARD DURING SUMMER | POPULAR | FAMILY FRIENDLY

Swim at the sandy beach or explore the rocks around the headland to Port Oriel – look for the remains of Red Man's Cave and perhaps even hear the ghost as he whistles and walks.

BY CAR: Heading south of Dundalk on the M1. Exit at Junction 12 onto the R170 to Clogherhead, parking at the beach. Alternatively, park at the harbour at Port Oriel, climb over the stile to the right of the harbour wall and starfish, and take the grassy track around the headland.

Grid refs:
Clogherhead Beach: O 16446 83569
Port Oriel: O 17010 84547

TIPS FOR WINTER SWIMMING

WHAT TO EXPECT

Your toes will feel extremely cold, perhaps sore, but don't worry: after a little while they will go numb and not hurt any more! Your breathing will be short and tight. Focus on the out-breath and swim first with your head up. When you put your face in, your cheeks may burn with the cold and an ice headache might take grip. Wear two caps or even a crazy woolly hat if you want to keep your head up. After a while, your hands will stop feeling the water properly and you may find that your little finger stretches out to the side and no amount of mental force will entice it back into line (this is one of my key indicators that it's time to get out).

EAR PLUGS

These help to keep the ears dry and stop that cold trickle seeping into the ear mid swim, They also protect you from developing the dreaded 'swimmer's ear'.

TAKE YOUR TIME GETTING IN

Walk in and allow your body to adjust. In very cold water your breathing will shorten and quicken, and your chest and neck can feel tight. Focus on breathing out long, slow breaths and you will settle. You may want to swim head up at first as you adjust your breathing and get used to the cold.

JOIN A FESTIVE CHARITY DIP

Charity dips are great for moral support and camaraderie – woolly hats are positively encouraged, and mulled wine and mince pies are a welcome after dip treat.

GET OUT BEFORE YOU'VE HAD ENOUGH

It is so much better to get out thinking, 'I'd like to get back in', rather than, 'That was awful, I never want to do it again.'

Facing page: Starfish sculpture at Port Oriel, County Louth

TIPS FOR NIGHT SWIMMING

Swimming by moonlight is a particularly magical experience; to swim into the silvery thread of water lit up by a full moon with the foreboding unknown darkness surrounding that faint glimmer of light is a surreal adventure. Highlight this beautiful experience with a small group of like-minded friends.

To get the full benefit requires a little advance preparation. Things look very different in the dark so choose a site you are familiar with and a swim buddy you are confident in.

Decide the boundaries of your swimming area and bring a lantern torch or bright glow sticks to mark your entry and exit point – ensure you stay within the visual limits of this light.

If this is a silent dip under a full moon there is no need for swimmers to wear glow sticks on their person. If, however, this is a training swim or even a large group of swimmers, it is very good practice to use glow sticks. My personal preference is to tuck the stick under the goggle strap at the back of my head. Some swimmers tie a length of string and tow the stick around their waist – the choice is yours. Glow sticks are readily available in outdoor and fishing stores.

If you are going for a long night swim with boat and kayak cover, remind the boat crew that if a torch is shone directly on the swimmer, the blinding light is all they will see. Again glow sticks taped to the nose and bow of the boat will help the swimmer travel in the right direction, and near the paddle blades allows the swimmer to gauge their distance in order not to get clipped.

Finally, at night-time the air temperature is considerably lower than during the day so bring extra-warm clothing, hot drinks, even have a barbeque (if it is permitted) and save any alcohol for the after-swim celebrations.

UNDER NO CIRCUMSTANCES SHOULD YOU SWIM AFTER TAKING ANY ALCOHOL

TIPS FOR FRONT CRAWL

A few lessons will do wonders for your confidence and skills. Here are some general tips:

BREATHE OUT UNDERWATER and practice breathing bilaterally, as breathing to both sides creates a more balanced stroke and means you can breathe away from wind and waves if necessary.

AIM FOR A LONG STROKE, stretch your arm forward before starting to pull and finish the stroke near the hip. Try to travel as far as you can with each stroke, but not necessarily to move the arms as quickly as you can.

SPOT WHERE YOU ARE GOING. Lifting your eyes to look forward regularly during your swim will keep you on course: in the sea, rivers and lakes there are no black lines to follow. 'Crocodile eyes' is a technique that allows you to spot and then drop your head back into the water without breaking the rhythm of your stroke (because you keep your eyes low over the water, like a crocodile). Practise this technique in the pool and in open water choose an object easy to see, for example; a church spire.

KICK YOUR LEGS. Although it does not provide a lot of propulsion in front crawl, kicking will help to lift the legs higher in the water, thereby giving you a more horizontal body position. This creates less drag and makes swimming much easier.

Men's legs tend to drag more than women's and when the waves are coming from behind many men feel they are being pushed down, where women have the advantage of almost surfing along the waves. A strong kick can help to lift the legs to this more advantageous position.

DEVELOP A HIGH ELBOW RECOVERY. Keeping the arm high on the recovery (over the water phase of the stroke) helps ensure your hands will clear the water in choppy conditions.

SWIM HEAD-UP FRONT CRAWL, water-polo style: this is a useful drill to increase kick power, the high elbow technique and looking forward, a three-in-one drill!

Practise your skills in the pool and then develop them in the open water.

Many leisure swimmers prefer swimming breaststroke or sidestroke (one of the lifesaving strokes, performed head up with a scissor-kick action). These are the easiest strokes to use if you want to have a conversation, take photos or take in the scenery.

TIPS FOR BODY SURFING

Body surfing can be great fun and utterly exhausting, the energy used to sprint in front of the drawing wave and then the exhilarating rush of white water boiling around your shoulders as you ride the breaking crest towards the beach. Be prepared to be tossed and tumbled as you try to regain your feet before the next wave rushes to meet the shore.

GETTING INTO THE SEA THROUGH WAVES

Present as little surface area to the breaker as possible and try to avoid swimming through the white water by diving through the breaking wave.

GETTING OUT OF THE SEA THROUGH WAVES

Catch the top of the wave and 'body surf' in; keep your arms in front of you and be careful of strong waves on steeply shelving beaches where the strong downward force can 'dump' the swimmer. Do not body surf in these conditions.